EXAMININ

Examinations are deeply emb
the career prospects of million:
University of Cambridge Loc
Cambridge Assessment, was at
lic examinations for schools wi ⌄ ⌄.ɑɩɩuards
in education. *Examining the Wc* ⌄ʌμɩɑɩns how the organisation, established in 1858, has evolved into a world authority on
assessment with three distinct areas of operation: international
examinations, UK examinations and English examinations for
Speakers of Other Languages. This is the first full-length history of the organisation, describing the development of its examinations from the early days to their present form, by authors
associated with Cambridge Assessment and other parts of the
University. It sets the history of the Cambridge Local Examinations Syndicate in its institutional context as a department of the
University and in the immense changes which have taken place
in examining in the UK and the wider world.

EXAMINING THE WORLD

A HISTORY OF THE
UNIVERSITY OF CAMBRIDGE
LOCAL EXAMINATIONS SYNDICATE

EDITED BY

SANDRA RABAN

Trinity Hall, Cambridge

CAMBRIDGE
UNIVERSITY PRESS

CAMBRIDGE UNIVERSITY PRESS
Cambridge, New York, Melbourne, Madrid, Cape Town, Singapore, São Paulo, Delhi

Cambridge University Press
The Edinburgh Building, Cambridge CB2 8RU, UK

Published in the United States of America by Cambridge University Press, New York

www.cambridge.org
Information on this title: www.cambridge.org/9780521709422

First published 2008

Printed in the United Kingdom at the University Press, Cambridge

A catalogue record for this publication is available from the British Library

ISBN 978-0-521-88414-3 hardback
ISBN 978-0-521-70942-2 paperback

*To all Cambridge candidates
past and present and future*

Contents

APPENDICES

ILLUSTRATIONS

Archival references are to the Cambridge Assessment Archive.

MAP

CONTRIBUTORS

SANDRA RABAN is Emeritus Fellow of Trinity Hall, Cambridge, and a former UCLES Syndic.

ELISABETH LEEDHAM-GREEN is the former Deputy Keeper of the Cambridge University Archives.

ANDREW WATTS has worked on national tests for 14-year-olds and the Cambridge Assessment Network for Cambridge Assessment since 1992.

HELEN PATRICK is a former research officer and senior research consultant with UCLES.

JOHN PATRICK is a historian and former teacher in the Aberdeen College of Education.

GREG LACEY is the former History Subject Officer and Officer in Charge of IGCSE with UCLES. He is currently a trainer and senior examiner with Cambridge Assessment.

PETER FALVEY is a former officer with the British Council and has spent some years seconded to UCLES as an English Language specialist and teacher education adviser. He is currently a part-time consultant with Cambridge ESOL.

GILLIAN COOKE has been the Group Archivist with Cambridge Assessment since 1996.

FOREWORD

I am grateful to Sandra Raban and her fellow contributors who, with the support of our Archivist Gillian Cooke, have put together this collection of essays to commemorate the 150th anniversary of the establishment in 1858 of the University of Cambridge Local Examinations Syndicate, now known as Cambridge Assessment.

It is, of course, quite possible to be educated without being examined, but the reality during the 150 years since the Syndicate's foundation is that public examinations and the experience of them have become an almost universal phenomenon. The memory of the row of desks in the school room on a hot summer afternoon, the anxiety and anticipation and then the surge of adrenalin as the paper is turned over, all these are part of the common currency of modern life, an experience shared beyond culture, time and place.

Some of the credit for this (if credit is due) belongs to Cambridge Assessment. Now, 150 years after its establishment, it sets and marks over 8 million examinations in 150 countries around the world, the only awarding body still owned by a university, and very much a global force in education. As such it serves the University's educational outreach, allowing Cambridge to engage with millions of learners around the world and to impact positively on their education.

This has always been a hallmark of the Cambridge approach and is one of the reasons the Syndicate has survived for 150 years and stayed true to its original purpose. This book describes how that has happened and how in the modern world, where we face the prospect of pen and paper exams finally giving way to computer-based tests, Cambridge's commitment to support all that is best in education means that it continues to be a progressive force, committed to modernisation, at the forefront of innovation and, in all its endeavours, devoted to the service and promotion of learning.

Simon Lebus
Group Chief Executive, Cambridge Assessment

1 Simon Lebus, Group Chief Executive, Cambridge Assessment, 2002 (photograph by Bruce Robertson, Cameo Photography)

Abbreviations

A level	Advanced level of the General Certificate of Education
A2	Second half of an A level qualification post-2000
AS	Advanced Supplementary Examination equivalent to half an A level
CIE	Cambridge International Examinations
CPE	Certificate of Proficiency in English
EFL	English as a Foreign Language
ESOL	English for Speakers of Other Languages
FCE	First Certificate in English
GCE	General Certificate of Education
GCSE	General Certificate of Secondary Education
IELTS	International English Language Testing Service
IGCSE	International General Certificate of Secondary Education
LEA	Local education authority
O level	Ordinary level of the General Certificate of Education
OCR	Oxford, Cambridge and RSA Examinations
RSA	Royal Society of Arts
UCLES	University of Cambridge Local Examinations Syndicate

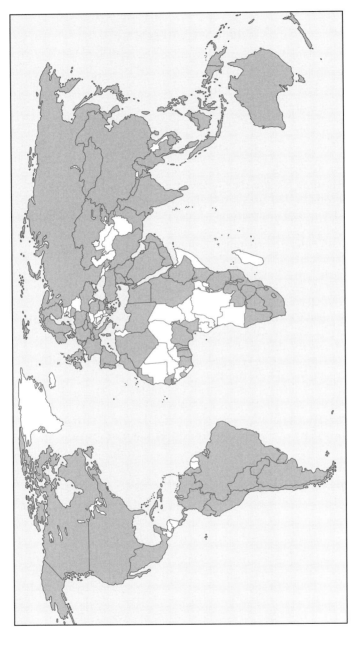

Map 1 Countries (shaded) where Cambridge Assessment had centres in 2006.

INTRODUCTION

SANDRA RABAN

For the first time, in 1858, 370 school candidates in 7 English cities sat examinations set by Cambridge University. Today this has risen to more than 8 million candidates a year in over 150 countries. The following chapters recount how such a remarkable expansion came about. Surprisingly perhaps, no one has attempted to do this before, other than in a handful of short articles, notably that of A. J. Stockwell who considered the first century of Cambridge overseas examining in the context of the British Empire. The 150th anniversary of the foundation of the organisation would seem to be an appropriate occasion to rectify the omission and celebrate its extraordinary success.

It is not a tale of inexorable growth. Although candidate numbers increased steadily over time, there were some major falterings and crises along the way, as well as a fair measure of luck. English language examinations would never have assumed such prominence had English not emerged as the world's second language during the course of the later twentieth century. On a smaller scale, it was sheer good fortune which found Cambridge well placed to assume responsibility for examining the whole of Zimbabwe when it gained independence because it had been examiner to the black rather than the white schools. The impact of the two world wars is evident in the following pages. Less evident, but deeply threatening nonetheless, was the economic dislocation of the early 1970s. The Local Examinations Syndicate, like the University Press and countless other organisations, found their financial stability undermined. It was generally rumoured that Frank Wild, Secretary from 1972 to 1983, had been charged by the University with either turning the organisation round or winding it up. Since then, it has shown a chameleon-like capacity to reinvent itself. The challenge of the post-colonial environment has been embraced with enthusiasm as have the opportunities presented by the growth of information technology – the latter not without its hiccoughs. In many parts of the world Cambridge has become a brand name synonymous with examinations, so much so that a possibly apocryphal story records that someone was once overheard asking whether a candidate was sitting 'Cambridge Cambridge or London Cambridge'. As in the rest of the world, the situation in England has seen radical changes in recent decades. Here the challenge of greater government intervention and a dizzying array of new examinations has been met with adaptability. Now Cambridge works in increasingly active partnership with its clients, becoming a leading player in curriculum development and the introduction of more sophisticated methods of assessment. The recent change of name to Cambridge Assessment bears witness to this capacity to build on past achievements while belonging quintessentially to the world of the future.

The following chapters describe different aspects of what has become a huge enterprise: the largest assessment agency in Europe. They begin with an account of Cambridge Assessment, now – as at its inception – a University department. As well as the Vice-Chancellor's signature which for many years appeared on certificates and the interest shown by HRH the Duke of Edinburgh, the University Chancellor, this affiliation explains the organisation's original title of the University of Cambridge Local Examinations Syndicate (UCLES). Always a mouthful, it was quaintly shortened to 'the Locals' by older generations of academics within Cambridge. Not surprisingly, outsiders found it incomprehensible and invented some imaginative alternatives. Letters arrived addressed to 'UNCLES' and the 'Locals Scheme Syndicate' or even, in desperation, 'To any Teacher, Cambridge, England'. In an article in *Education Guardian* in August 1988, it was hailed as the 'University of Cambridge Language Education System', which at least matched the UCLES abbreviation. To those who worked for the organisation, it was known simply as 'the Syndicate', regardless of the fact that Cambridge was littered with syndicates overseeing University bodies directly responsible to the Council. Small wonder that it was thought time to move to something simpler and more self-explanatory. For the purposes of this history, however,

2 HRH the Duke of Edinburgh, Chancellor of the University, with John Reddaway, the Secretary, and Jim Jones, the Operations Manager, at the Syndicate in 1993 (*UCLES Annual Review,* 1993)

'the Syndicate' has generally been preferred to 'Cambridge Assessment' since this would have been the normal usage during the period it covers.

A word should also be said about acronyms. The world of examining is more than usually afflicted by acronymphomania. Indeed, when serving as a Syndic (see chapter 1), I was equipped with an impressively substantial compilation of those in current use. In order to make life easier for readers for whom the majority will be unfamiliar, contributors have exercised extreme restraint and confined themselves to the few commonly recognised acronyms provided in the list of abbreviations. Otherwise, the existence of an acronym is merely noted after the full name on its first appearance.

At first glance it might seem curious that Cambridge University has become responsible for the assessment of so many millions of candidates who are not its own students. It is, however, very much part of its remit as an international institution. The relationship is fundamentally symbiotic. The involvement of academics as examiners from the Syndicate's earliest days has been mutually beneficial. If they were often driven by a concern for standards in order to ensure that future students arrived well prepared, the University also benefited from familiarity with what was happening elsewhere in the educational system, whether in England or abroad. The Syndicate itself gained access to a huge range of expertise within the University, a resource more important in the past before modern communications and localisation made it possible to tap this talent in the country where it was needed. The Syndicate has also played a vital role in creating the University Trust Funds which enable so many overseas students of modest means to study in Cambridge.

Chapter 2 describes the early years of the Syndicate, followed by chapters detailing more recent work at home, overseas and in the specialised area of examining English for speakers of other languages. Varied though the different aspects of the Syndicate's activities are, several themes recur time and time again as one reads the accounts of each aspect of its activities. The University has always felt a strong commitment to the maintenance of standards and the promotion of good practice within the secondary school system. In the early years it played an instrumental role in this. Today much of the responsibility has been assumed by governments at home and abroad, but examining bodies remain the principal source of research into refining methods of assessment and developing new ones.

Comparability was a word which made an early appearance in Syndicate affairs, whether it was comparability over time, comparability between the standards of different UK examining boards, comparability between different subjects within the same Board or parity between the standards of examinations taken in different countries. All these issues have become the more crucial as the 'one size fits all' examinations of the past have given way to a plethora of syllabuses and papers geared to the needs of candidates of varying abilities and a wide range of cultures. Present-day pupils worldwide no longer have to study Anglo-centric syllabuses, which were all that was available to them in the days when home and overseas candidates sat exactly the same examinations. Examiners as well as methods of assessment are now monitored in increasingly sophisticated and sensitive ways. No longer is the mere possession of a Cambridge degree a sufficient guarantee of competence or probity. Drawn from a far wider background and with appropriate experience, examiners now receive specialised training and supervision. Greater involvement of teachers at all stages in the assessment process has helped in its professionalisation. A happy result of this more collaborative approach has been to enable candidates to demonstrate what they can do rather than merely to expose their shortcomings.

From the beginning, the Syndicate regarded the syllabus as important as assessment itself. This is what principally distinguished the English tradition of examining, based on essays, from the psychometric approach exemplified by the Educational Testing Service at Princeton in the USA. Testing understanding and skills by means of essays has proved far more difficult than testing knowledge, which relied heavily on multiple-choice questions and permitted a high degree of consistency between results from one examination to the next. Much work has been done in recent years to ensure the validity of the Cambridge approach, in addition to the adoption of tests emphasising reliability. The chief manifestation of this has been the emergence of English language tests comparable to those of the Educational Testing Service alongside older suites of examinations, which have themselves been revised. Now, the accent in examinations of all sorts is to draw on best practice from whatever tradition it comes, in order to provide for an ever wider range of clients, many of whom require tests for vocational purposes.

Syndics showed an early and concerned awareness of the importance of examination results to the future of candidates. In many countries a Cambridge certificate was the indispensable passport to a white-collar job. Today, paper qualifications are important to us all. One can thus understand the commitment of candidates worldwide to achieving success, often at high personal cost in terms of effort and expenditure. They are deservedly proud of their Cambridge certificates or diplomas. This was movingly demonstrated during the Second World War when examinations sometimes provided a vestige of normality and a goal to boost morale for prisoners of war. On the Home Front, the stoicism of pupils sitting their examinations throughout the London blitz is remarkable. So in its way is the fact that Cambridge examinations continued to be taken even in enemy territory. Assistant Secretary Jack Roach, recalling his visits to continental Europe at the end of 1939, recounted how:

My visit to Belgium in October 1939 had an indirect result that the examinations were maintained clandestinely throughout the war.

My visit to Italy at Christmas 1939 had a similar result. The nuns at Florence kept a present for me hidden under the dais of a room used by German troops and Sister Pauline at Rome kept the examinations going throughout the war – without the name Cambridge.

The integrity of the examinations has always been accorded the highest priority, not least because clients are attracted to Cambridge because of its internationally recognised standards and freedom from corruption. Complex measures were in place from an early date to ensure that question papers reached candidates unseen by third parties. It has long been Syndicate practice to ensure that replacement papers can be provided at short notice should security ever be breached. If necessary, papers can be reset speedily for examinations taken by many countries, as was indeed the case in 1981. Today, in a climate where the need for security has invaded everyday life to a level unimaginable only a few years ago, Cambridge Assessment has the full panoply of modern security arrangements in place.

The early Syndicate shared many of the best characteristics of Victorian public service. Devoted officers ensured that systems were in place and that examinations could run without hitches, come what may. As one can see from chapter 2, their ingenuity was often challenged, especially during the major upheavals of world war. In other respects, the record was less distinguished. Women were underrepresented to the point of complete absence at professional level until the 1950s. Marie Overton, who had studied at Newnham College, was appointed Assistant to the Secretaries in 1946 but, despite her educational background, the Syndics made it clear that the post was to be regarded as clerical. This did not change even though she went on to become Subject Officer for English, a responsibility normally entrusted to officers. The first true appointment at officer level was that of Jane Burchnall, appointed in 1954. Memorably, she married

Frank Wild, then a Syndic, whom she had met on an overseas visit, and subsequently resigned. As in so many other organisations of the day, women were numerous among what Cambridge calls 'the Assistant Staff', but they only multiplied at higher levels during the 1980s. Now, from the Chief Executive of Cambridge International Examinations (CIE) downwards, they play as prominent a role in the organisation as their male colleagues.

In the nature of things, the chiefs have always been better recorded than the 'injuns'. Over its 150-year existence, Cambridge Assessment has been singularly fortunate in the quality of those who have led it. This is the more surprising in that its Secretaries were never professional educationalists and came from a wide variety of academic backgrounds. Many had distinguished careers in other fields before or after taking office. Some appear time and again in the following pages. Such, for example, were Neville Keynes, father of Maynard, and Joseph Brereton who held office from 1945 to 1961. Jack Roach, who played a key role in the development of English language examinations and had been Brereton's bitter rival for the post of Secretary, went on to play an important role in Civil Service selection after he abandoned the Syndicate in disappointment. It should also be said that some of the early Secretaries and their Syndics, while steadfast in defence of the Syndicate's interests, showed the same intransigence in the face of change as that of the University at large, as described by Gordon Johnson in his introduction to Francis Cornford's *Microcosmographia Academica*, first published in 1908 – and also the same ability to turn defeat into triumph when change was forced upon them.

For all the devotion of Secretaries and staff, the organisation essentially resembled a cottage industry until the great expansion from the 1980s. The Secretaryship of Frank Wild was pivotal; the Syndicate might as easily have foundered. Instead it embarked upon a period of vigorous expansion and innovation in all its areas of operation, fostered by the entrepreneurial flair of his successor, John Reddaway. The appointment of specialists such as Peter Hargreaves from the British Council and the development of new examinations in English for speakers of other languages are detailed in Peter Falvey's chapter. Equally far-reaching developments took place in school examinations overseas, where the Syndicate became far more responsive to the needs of its clients. Greg Lacey shows how a vast range of modern assessments has been built on the foundations of the old colonial system. Specially designed suites of international examinations now operate alongside updated versions of older examinations such as School Certificate and O level, no longer available within England and Wales but for which there is a continuing demand abroad. Today the emphasis is on partnership with teachers and their ministries. It is striking how often nations share the same educational concerns the world over, irrespective of wealth or political persuasion, and there has been both pleasure and profit in working with the teaching profession in individual states to provide forms of assessment which meet their needs.

In England, as chapter 3 makes clear, increasing government intervention has left less room for initiative. The higher political profile of education is to be welcomed. No longer is the refrain 'Our children are our future' heard only on the lips of ministry officials from other countries. There is a real commitment to raising educational standards and providing assessment to match changes in the school curriculum. But there have been some casualties. It is no longer feasible to undertake the development of innovative syllabuses such as the Cambridge History Project. The somewhat frenetic pace at which new examinations have been introduced since the reforms set in motion by James Callaghan's Ruskin speech of 1976 has presented challenges which have sometimes stretched the Syndicate to its limits. So successful indeed was the Midland Examining Group, of which Cambridge was a member, in attracting candidates for the first GCSE examination in 1988, that John Reddaway, an engineer by academic discipline, called in structural engineers to assess whether the floors of Syndicate Buildings could bear the weight of the question papers. A key to the future of this aspect of Cambridge Assessment has been its ability to play a leading role in the rationalisation of examining bodies which took place principally in the last decade of the twentieth century. As Elisabeth Leedham-Green shows, this was in no small measure due to the wisdom of Cambridge University in allowing the Syndicate to accumulate and control its own financial reserves.

At the same time, the organisation itself had to make structural changes to cope with its increased activities and the need to absorb so many new partners in a short space of time. This task fell largely to Michael Halstead, appointed Chief Executive in 1993. The abandonment of the old title of Secretary, based on the Civil Service model, here, as elsewhere in the University, heralded a conscious move towards modern management methods. So too did the creation of separate business streams and employment arrangements outside those of the University. One might feel nostalgia for the days when the professional staff were all University officers and everyone worked from a single building, but the constraints this imposed were at too great a cost. The world had changed and the Syndicate had, perforce, to change with it.

All the contributors to this volume have brought to their chapters a wide experience of working with the Syndicate or, in the case of Elisabeth Leedham-Green, the University. Each chapter is a self-standing account of the Syndicate's history from their perspective. A special word of thanks is due from us all to Gillian Cooke, Archivist to Cambridge Assessment, on whom we have shamelessly relied for support and evidence. It is a great pleasure to me that she has been able to contribute the final chapter on research and development. We would also like to thank William Bickerdike, Sarah Deverell, Desmond Nicholson and the staff and students of the EF Language School, Cambridge, as well as staff of Cambridge Assessment too numerous to mention by name, but whose help has been no less appreciated. Michael Sharp, who showed a keen and supportive interest in the archives, would undoubtedly have been included among our thanks but for his untimely death.

All historians face problems of source material. Like many other organisations, Cambridge Assessment has only recently come to appreciate the importance of its records. The first professional Archivist was appointed in 1996. To describe the earliest records as unsystematic is to put it mildly. Not only have no minutes survived from the first Syndicate meetings, but it seems that none were kept. While Secretary Liveing destroyed many of his papers before his death, Keynes kept a commonplace book of oddities, examination howlers and bizarre correspondence. This strikes a lighter note than most of the contents of the Archive. Even more fascinating are the contents of what is known as 'The War Box', the source of many of the

3 The Rugby Centre box taken to examinations by the Presiding Examiner and
the abacus which was used in examination processing until 1976 (photograph
by Nigel Luckhurst)

more vivid details in the following pages. Alongside these curiosities,
there are copious records of routine business. These have expanded in
line with the organisation itself. Until 1947, everything for each year –
question papers, pass lists, examiners' reports, syllabuses, timetables,
circulars, the Annual Report and list of Secretaries – fitted into a single

small, if increasingly fat, book. By contrast, the records for 2004 fill 10 metres of shelving and that is without the statistics or results.

Precise comparisons over time are difficult. It is not always clear, for example, whether figures for home examinations refer to candidates or to subject entries, whether they include all candidates or only 16+ and 18+ candidates, whether they include all subjects or not, whether they include winter as well as summer examinations and whether they refer to England only or also include Wales and entries from elsewhere in the UK. There are also changes in 'accounting' practices. For example, the Syndicate counted a candidate making entries for both O level and A level as one candidate until 1960, when such a candidate began to be counted as two. As the contributors to the volume quickly came to appreciate, there is also much that never found its way onto paper at all. We have all drawn on oral memory, our own and that of others. The Archivist has also begun a collection of taped interviews while the actors in the drama of the more recent past are still with us.

Overall, there remains a rich harvest, both in the archives of Cambridge Assessment and in the Cambridge University Archives, which the following pages have barely touched upon. Cambridge Assessment is worthy of a full-length history to match that of the University Press, not only in institutional terms, but because public examinations have been so closely intertwined with society and the aspirations of its citizens since the mid nineteenth century. As the Nigerian educationalist A. A. Adeyinka put it when surveying the Syndicate's influence on the Nigerian educational system: 'The measurement of educational progress recorded by success in formal examinations and of educational tests . . . forms an indispensable part of the social and political life of a people'. Nigeria is only one of the many countries where Cambridge examinations have had a profound impact. It has been impossible to do them all justice in a volume of this length. Each has a story to match that of examination development in England and Wales. One hopes that a further century and a half will not pass before all this receives the attention it deserves.

1

THE UNIVERSITY

ELISABETH LEEDHAM-GREEN

Attention was called to the omission of any reference to the making of paper patterns in the new Needlework schedule.

Clearly a trivial question for a sub-sub-sub-Syndicate committee way
back in the 1880s. Wrong. In fact a matter considered by the full Syndicate on 27 February 1930, a time when, indeed, steps had recently
been taken to extend membership of the Syndicate to external members, but when individuals actively engaged in teaching and research
in the University were strongly represented. How much, we may wonder, did how many of them understand the not inconsiderable mys-
teries of the making of paper patterns?

Much of the first part of this chapter will be concerned with services done to the Syndicate by persons otherwise fully engaged in
the central business of the University and colleges, which persons,
it should be reported lest the suspense become unbearable, decided
that, in the Needlework schedule, questions relating to the making of
paper patterns should be optional – cynics might signal this as an early
example of 'dumbing-down', but how many readers have attempted
this devilish art?

In considering the Examinations Syndicate as a constituent part of
the University, comparisons beg to be made with similar, more or less
autonomous, bodies: the University Press, the Fitzwilliam Museum,
the Botanic Garden and, above all, the Board of Extra-Mural Studies (originally Local Lectures, now Continuing Education). Syndicates, in Cambridge parlance, are committees established to manage
or oversee particular aspects of the University's business, whether
of a permanent nature, like most of those mentioned in this chapter,

or temporary, such as those set up to deal with things like the erection of a new building, compliance with new legislation, and the like. Members are, typically, appointed by the University to serve for a set number of years and are known as Syndics.

From 1878 to 1925 Local Examinations and Local Lectures were managed by a single syndicate, but from early days there were notable differences in the nature of the University's commitment to the two enterprises – differences exemplified by the rôles of pioneers of these branches of what we would now call 'outreach' and what was then called University Extension.

THE EARLY YEARS

The founding father of the Local Lectures, James Stuart, was Professor of Mechanism and Applied Mechanics from 1875 to 1889, and had inaugurated the Cambridge Extension Lectures in 1873. He struggled to turn his subject from one for which only an ordinary degree could be achieved to one boasting an honours degree – a 'tripos' in the arcane language of Cambridge – which was not, in the event, to happen until 1894. His failure to achieve recognition for his subject was, partly at least, responsible for his resignation of his chair, and he went on to concentrate on his career in national politics (MP for Hackney, 1884; for Hoxton, 1885–1900; for Sunderland, 1906–10) and, as a consequence of his marriage in 1890 to Laura Colman, daughter of the mustard magnate Sir Jeremiah Colman, to the directorship of Colman's Mustard until his death in 1913. His mantle was inherited by Richard Green Moulton, MA of Christ's in 1877, and Ph.D. of Pennsylvania in 1891, University Extension Lecturer from 1877 to 1890; and by Robert Davies Roberts, Fellow of Clare, 1884 to 1890, and Secretary of the Local Lectures Syndicate from 1894 to 1902. All three both lectured and published copiously on their particular subjects and on the topic of university extension. After Stuart had left the University, and Roberts had resigned his lectureship in geology, which he held from 1883 to 1886, none of these three were intimately involved with the central concerns of the University.

By contrast, the early leading lights of the local examinations were mostly deeply embedded in university and/or college life. H. J. Roby,

Secretary of the Syndicate in 1859, it is true, left the University shortly afterwards to become Under-Master of Dulwich College, 1861–5; Professor of Jurisprudence at University College, London, 1866–8; Secretary to the Schools Inquiry and Endowed Schools Commissions, 1865–72; Commissioner of Endowed Schools, 1872–4; and, surprisingly, a cotton manufacturer and MP. His successor in 1860, John Fuller, was a Fellow of Emmanuel, 1848–63, and Tutor, 1850–63. George Liveing, who succeeded to the Secretaryship in 1861, on the other hand, was Professor of Chemistry from 1861 to 1908 and, allegedly, the first teacher of experimental science in the University. Furthermore, in the words of the *Alumni Cantabrigienses* compiled by J. and J. A. Venn, which gives biographical information about all members of the University from the earliest times to 1900: 'As the Cambridge correspondent of two successive Chancellors, Dukes of Devonshire, he discharged a task of considerable responsibility with strict impartiality and great industry, and with characteristic scrupulousness destroyed all the records of this before his death.'

Liveing's commitment to the local examinations was remarkable. He was an examiner for the first examinations in Chemistry, Electricity and Magnetism, and also conducted the examinations at Liverpool; the following year he cheerfully examined the preliminary subjects and English. His term of office as Secretary over, he served intermittently as a Syndic for another thirteen years between 1863 and 1894.

Every one of the examiners in 1859 either was already or was subsequently to become distinguished in the University. One was already Dean of Ely, one was already a professor (Sterndale Bennett, Professor of Music) and a further six were to achieve chairs later – in most cases, not much later – in their careers. Two were to become heads of house (principals, under various titles, of one or other of the colleges to which all students at the University must belong). Nor did such elevation remove them from the scene. In 1860, H. W. Cookson, Master of Peterhouse, examined botany and geology, and in 1871, Liveing, although not at the time a Syndic, was still examining. For the first few years, indeed, the examiners for all subjects are listed at the very least as Fellows or past Fellows of colleges, with the early exception of drawing, which was allotted to a member of staff of one of the London technical institutions, as were, in due course, some of the commercial

4 George Downing Liveing, Honorary Secretary from 1861 to 1862
(Cambridge Assessment)

subjects which the Syndicate was empowered to examine from 1888. In 1873, for example, of forty-one subject examiners, twenty-three were Fellows, eleven lately Fellows, one a professor and one a college lecturer, and all but the examiner of drawing (from the School of Art, Kensington) were Cambridge MAs. Eleven of them also served as Presiding Examiners (i.e. invigilators). Of these last there were sixty-five, including thirty-one Fellows and twelve late Fellows. To these were shortly added three women – Mrs Liveing in Cambridge, the Hon. Mrs Atkinson in Manchester and Mrs Roby in London – for the invigilation of female students.

The great majority of Syndics either examined or conducted examinations or both. Several of them had been members of the University's Council of the Senate when it accepted the original proposals for local examinations in November 1857 and set up the first permanent syndicate in the following month. It was very much a 'hands-on' operation.

The involvement in the exercise of so many distinguished members of the University indicates at the very least the importance the University attached to the standard of teaching in schools – naturally enough, as it hoped to attract its share of the cream of the school leavers. At the same time, the association of the University, as also of Oxford, with the earliest examinations lent them a status likely to commend them to schools.

As to the technical and commercial subjects, their place in the Cambridge Board's scheme of things tended to dwindle, although they never entirely disappeared, until the shake-up of national examination schemes and the related merger with the Royal Society of Arts examinations at the end of 1997 brought them back within the newly extended fold.

Of the very earliest years no detailed account can be given. Hands were not only on, but kept close to the chest. The earliest meeting for which minutes survive was that of 11 December 1862 in a volume subsequently used for rough memoranda. The first formal minute book starts with the meeting of 13 January 1866, and bears a note stating that 'No minutes were kept before Mr Gray's secretaryship' (i.e. from 1863). The approval of earlier minutes is not mentioned in the first entries for either volume. It appears, however, that the offices of Honorary Secretary and Honorary Treasurer rotated annually at first. Thus the minutes for 24 March 1863 record that 'The accounts made out by Professor Liveing were audited and the vouchers examined.'

The careers of the first known of these rotating Secretaries – Roby, Fuller and Liveing – are outlined above. The year 1862 saw two Secretaries, the Revd A. Hobson of St John's, then Assistant University Librarian, and R. Potts of Trinity, a private coach in Cambridge and the author of very successful mathematical textbooks. His successor, Charles Gray, Fellow, Assistant Tutor and Junior Dean of Trinity, served from 1863 until 1866 when he took up the living of East

Retford, Nottinghamshire, as a prelude to a modestly successful eccle-
siastical career. He was followed by the Revd Thomas Markby of
Trinity, previously headmaster of a proprietary school at St John's
Wood, London, and now living in Cambridge as a coach and as Classical Lecturer at Trinity Hall. On his death in 1869 he was succeeded by
George Forrest Browne, Fellow of St Catharine's, lately Mathematical Master at Trinity College, Glenalmond, in Scotland (1857–63).
Neither Gray nor Markby were particularly conspicuous within the
University but this fact perhaps reflects the perceived need for a full-
time senior administrator for the conduct of the Syndicate's business –
something, as it turned out, not to be achieved until Neville Keynes'
resignation in 1910.

From his return to Cambridge in 1863 Browne became a local colossus. He served St Catharine's College as Fellow, Chaplain, Lecturer
and Tutor; and the University as proctor, one of two officers with dis-
ciplinary and ceremonial duties (1869, 1877 and 1879); as first Editor
of the *Cambridge University Reporter*, the University's official gazette,
on its launch in 1870; as Lady Margaret Preacher, 1878; as Secretary
of the University Commission, 1877–81; and as Disney Professor of
Archaeology (1887–92). He was a member of Selwyn College Council from 1886 to 1930. He departed from Cambridge to a canonry at
St Paul's Cathedral (1892–7), followed by the suffragan bishopric of
Stepney (1895–7) and the bishopric of Bristol (1897–1914). He was
a founder Fellow of the British Academy (1903), Chairman of the
Church Historical Society, President of the Alpine Club (1905), a JP
for Cambridge and a member of the town council. He was also, from
1869 to 1875, Rector of Ashley-cum-Silverley in Cambridgeshire,
near the Suffolk border, about 14 miles (22 km) from Cambridge as
the crow flies, about half as much again by road.

Somehow, in the midst of all this, he served as a highly successful
Secretary of the Local Examinations Syndicate from 1861 and, after
the merger in 1878, of the Local Examinations and Lectures Syndicate
until 1892. Given the extent of his activities it is not surprising, though
it is disappointing, that Browne does not devote more space in his
autobiography to his years as Secretary to the Syndicate, although it
is telling that he states 'that for some twenty-one years it was the most
important, in my judgment, of the offices which were entrusted to me

by the University', and this in spite of having, apart from the offices enumerated above, served on the Council of the Senate for eighteen years starting in 1874.

If Browne's account of his Secretaryship is sparse, it can be supplemented by the diaries of Neville Keynes (father of the celebrated economist Maynard Keynes), Assistant Secretary from 1881, Secretary for Local Examinations from 1892 (when a separate secretary was appointed for the Local Lectures) and, from 1911, University Registrary, the principal administrative officer of the University. He was for most of this time concurrently Bursar of Pembroke College, Secretary to the University Council and lecturing and publishing on political economy.

Although Keynes found Browne, initially at least, 'a very pleasant man to work with', he did not remain uncritical. He writes on several occasions, not always sympathetically, of Browne's long-deferred hopes of ecclesiastical preferment, and records, as the transfer of responsibility approached: 'With a view to the future I have this year been attending the Local Examinations audit. It seems to me that in this department, as in others, a good deal would be gained if G. F. B were more methodical.' Browne also acquired a reputation for high-handedness: 'In the Local Lectures Annual Report G. F. B is proposing without a word of warning or – as far as I can make out – consulting a single person to subsidise Agricultural Chemistry to the extent of £150 a year. I feel inclined to protest strongly.' The signs had been perceived earlier:

This week we are having meetings of Sections. Today at the Junior English, Browne was asking solemnly, 'shall the section decide absolutely for such and such a standard or shall it be left to the discretion of the office?' Beck broke in with, 'Well, of course, we know that the Office will in any case do just what it likes' – a statement which contained enough of the truth to cause some merriment.

Already, then, there was an uneasiness about the extent to which the Syndicate's officers, with the more or less tacit approval of the Syndics, were free to operate as a body only nominally associated with the University at large.

Secretaries were appointed by a panel of senior academics under the chairmanship of the Vice-Chancellor. By today's standards,

5 George Forrest Browne, Secretary from 1870 to 1892 (Cambridge Assessment)

procedures were somewhat ramshackle and, according to a memoir by Jack Roach written forty years after the event, left a great deal to be desired. He and Joseph Brereton, both Assistant Secretaries, had been rival candidates to succeed Nalder Williams as Secretary in 1945. His account etches in acid his view of the selection process, Brereton's shortcomings and the judgement of the then Vice-Chancellor. Faced with two strong and unyielding candidates, a Joint Secretaryship was proposed. Although the memoir is a testament to decades of brooding resentment, it does appear that the matter was ineptly handled and that two men of such different temperaments would not have made

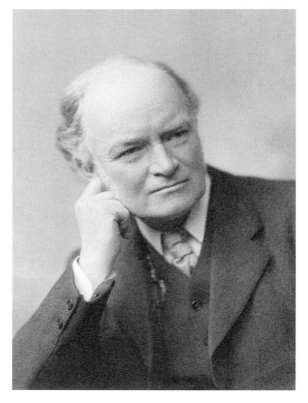

6 John Neville Keynes, Secretary from 1892 to 1910 (Cambridge Assessment)

a successful partnership. Happily for all concerned, Roach decided to accept a post with the Civil Service Commission working along-side C. P. Snow to set up the Civil Service Selection Board, a body mercilessly lampooned in A. P. Herbert's *Number Nine: or the Mind-Sweepers* (1951).

If Browne was a colossus, giants on the Syndicate were not want-ing. Professor Liveing has already been mentioned, but the exertions of others were hardly less strenuous. Henry Montagu Butler (Master of Trinity, 1886–1918) had been a member of the original Syndicate and one of the first examiners. He subsequently left Cambridge to become Headmaster of Harrow and then Dean of Gloucester, but on his return he quickly took up the reins once more and served on the Syndicate from 1888 for many years, including the last ten years of his life. Other committed Syndics who were or were subsequently to become heads of houses included W. H. Bateson (Master of St John's College, 1857–81), W. M. Campion (President of Queens' College, 1892–6), Henry Latham (Master of Trinity Hall, 1888–1902) and S. G. Phear (Master of Emmanuel College, 1871–95). All were also active on numerous other syndicates. No less distinguished have been the Syndics of the present day, but they have not been called upon to set, mark and invigilate examinations as their earliest forebears did, nor yet to inspect schools.

By the time of Browne's appointment the decision had already been made to admit girls to the local examinations, and from then on the causes of university extension and of the education of women were to be closely entwined, although some individuals were more committed to one cause than the other as the 'thin edge of the wench' was debated. It was the Syndicate which officially administered the examinations not only of the first women students in Cambridge but of all such, as they were not members of the University until 1948, when women were admitted to full membership. Although this was only a technicality, as the final examinations were set – and, albeit unofficially, marked – by the official University examiners, the mechanics of administration served to keep the Syndicate close to an intermittently central concern of the University. Moreover, the examination fees payable by women students contributed significantly to the Syndicate's income: a typical example of the Syndicate 'doing well by doing good' in the immortal words of Tom Lehrer.

CONSTITUTION

The Syndicate as originally constituted comprised, as we have seen, twelve members of the Regent House (the resident members of the University holding university or college posts), under the chairmanship of the Vice-Chancellor. In 1918 there was established a Joint Committee for Examinations, which included, in addition to seven Syndics who were members of the Regent House, two members each from the Associations for Headmasters and Headmistresses and one each from the Association of Assistant Masters and Assistant Mistresses of Private Schools. Ten or so years later, in response to external suggestions that there was a need for more direct contact between the University and the schools which it examined, and which supplied its students, the number of Syndics appointed by the Regent House was reduced from the then fifteen to twelve, and they were henceforth to serve a term of four years rather than five. To these were added four external Syndics: one man and one woman engaged in school teaching and two others to be appointed from the ranks of Local Education Officers or His Majesty's Inspectors of Schools. By this time the rival examining bodies – the Oxford and Cambridge Joint Board, the Oxford Local Examinations Delegacy, and the Northern Universities Joint Matriculation Board – all had external representation.

This early example of appointing Syndics who were not resident members of the University, paralleled only by the Appointments Board (now the Careers Service Syndicate), prefigures developments in more recent years. It was not, however, to be a permanent arrangement. Between 1982 and 2001, for example, the Syndics again comprised only resident members of the University, selected largely with a view to their academic field and their ability to chair the meetings of the various subject-committees, although external representatives were present on many, if not all, committees. As central government took responsibility from the mid 1980s for setting the school syllabus, and as the Syndicate's overseas work increased, both in setting and administering international school examinations and, particularly, in English Language testing, the Syndics were required to act rather as a board of directors, and occasionally as ambassadors to overseas clients, than as arbiters of academic standards. This was all the more necessary because of the vast expansion in national school and vocational examining following the amalgamation with other boards, including the Royal Society of Arts, as related in chapter 3. The old-style subject specialist supervision undertaken by the Syndicate now took place in the Council for Home Examinations, a consultative rather than a hands-on body.

PRESENT CONSTITUTION

The amalgamations were partly the product of government pressure which had necessitated an even greater degree of collaboration between the various examining bodies. Cambridge, by now one of the largest and most successful of such bodies by virtue of its overseas and English Language examinations, and with considerable control of its reserves, in appropriate accordance with Newtonian physics duly attracted the smaller.

Revision of the composition of the Syndicate itself was not the only change brought about by the huge increase in the scale of the organisation's activities: turnover had increased threefold between 1985 and 1992. As is not uncommon when the head of a large body is approaching retirement, a review committee was set up by the University in 1991 in order to assess the aims and objectives of the Syndicate; the relationship of the organisation and its staff to the University; the mechanism for regulating its reserves; and the qualities desirable in a successor to John Reddaway, the then Secretary.

As its terms of reference portended, Reddaway proved to be the last of the old-style academic administrators recruited to run the Syndicate. His successor, Michael Halstead, although a research chemist with Shell earlier in his career, came from the Old Schools where he had been University Treasurer since 1985. His successor, Simon Lebus, appointed in 2002, was the first to come from a career in business. Likewise, the re-naming of the Secretary as Chief Executive at the end of John Reddaway's period in office, in parallel with the Press and in accordance with the usual terminology for the leader of a major enterprise, signified the University's appreciation of the vastly increased scope of the Syndicate's activities, its now very numerous staff and its international profile.

In the event, most of the recommendations of the review committee concerned the treatment of the Syndicate's reserves and greater oversight of its activities by the University's Council through the introduction of an agreed five-year rolling plan. The proposals were deplored, very effectively, by the Syndicate's sole representative on the committee, who pointed out the dangers of political intervention in commercial judgements. These sentiments were endorsed and amplified by a response to the committee's report by Reddaway stressing *inter alia* the Syndicate's need to make quick decisions in reaction to world events (such as the break-up of the Soviet Union and developments in China and in South Africa), and therefore the lack

7 Michael Halstead, Chief Executive from 1993 to 2002, visiting Garden
International School, Kuala Lumpur (*UCLES Annual Review*, 1997)

of realism in the suggestion that the Syndicate should be tied to an
agreed rolling plan. The Syndics for their part were adamant that
they should have control of any rolling plan and the reserves and that
they should be permitted to 'exercise authority as well as responsibility'. In the event, the degree of control which the Syndicate had
over its operations and reserves was maintained. The final clauses in
the University Statute governing Cambridge Assessment continue to
provide for an Annual Report from the Syndicate to the Council and
that no transfer of funds should be made without the agreement of the

Syndics. Sir Geoffrey Cass, Chief Executive of the Press, was asked to advise on the level of reserves appropriate to an organisation of the size of the Syndicate and there the matter rested.

The question of the use of the Syndicate's reserves had a long history. From the 1890s the Syndicate was beginning to be seen as a convenient milch-cow, not only for the nurture of the local examinations and local lectures but for the University at large. For example, when a central property came onto the market, the University authorities, while having no immediate use for it, but anxious to acquire a prime site, would persuade the Syndicate to purchase it, nearly always seriously overestimating the rental value. Thus, in 1892, Kenmare House (74 Trumpington Street) and 1 Mill Lane were acquired, shortly to be joined by 75 Trumpington Street (to be taken over by the military authorities in 1918 as a meat store), then leased to the Board of Architectural Studies, and, on their terminating the lease in 1925, leased to F. T. Cross of Ely as a restaurant. So much for the then pressing needs of the University for accommodation.

Some contributions to the University's real estate, however, bore more directly on its core business: for example, in February 1906 the Syndicate agreed to contribute £1,500 to the building of the Examination Halls, with the proviso that the rooms would be suitable and available for Summer Meeting purposes (for the Local Lectures sessions); in 1917 and 1919 it made substantial contributions to the costs of building the Mill Lane Lecture Rooms; in January 1925 it agreed to pay, out of the balance of the Admission of Women account, the two remaining instalments of the loan incurred for the building of the Chemical Laboratory; in May 1932 it contributed £2,000 towards the repair of the Temperate and Palm Houses at the Botanic Garden, a facility for all residents in and visitors to the city, and for many years the provider of specimens for practical examinations in botany.

There is thus a long history to the Syndicate's contributions to the University's general funds but the terms on which it has made them have changed over time. At a meeting with representatives of the Financial Board in October 1936 it was stressed that 'while it would be proper for the Syndicate on any occasion to make suggestions to the University on the allocation of any money which the Syndicate might offer for University purposes, the decision must rest with the

University'. To a considerable extent the situation described above has continued to the present day, but there has been greater sensitivity as to how the funds should be employed. The Syndicate's surpluses have from time to time provided very welcome contributions to the University Chest (£121 million in the last quarter of a century) and have increasingly been made over to University causes directly relevant to the Syndicate's work. Thus, when the Cambridge Commonwealth Trust was established in 1982 (to be followed in 1988 by the Cambridge Overseas Trust) to provide funding for (mainly) post-graduate students who could not otherwise afford to come to Cambridge, the Syndicate contributed £10 million in the first year and a further £8 million to these two trusts thereafter, so furthering the educational opportunities of students who may very well have gained their earlier qualifications via the Syndicate's International examinations. By 2004, nearly 11,000 students had benefited from awards from these two trusts. In addition, £3 million have gone to establish the Research Centre for English and Applied Linguistics, with obvious relevance to the examinations in English for Speakers of Other Languages which make up one of the three main streams of the Syndicate's activities. There have also been annual subventions to the graduate colleges in Cambridge for the support of students from countries where the Syndicate's overseas work is focused.

Although the Syndicate has been in a position to make financial contributions to the University from time to time, it should not be forgotten that, as a University department, the University also remains liable for any losses should the organisation founder. This is no empty obligation. In the 1970s when many British enterprises were in sore need of modernisation, and international economic conditions were unstable, both the Press and the Examinations Syndicate gave rise to serious concern on the part of the University authorities. The crisis at the Press has been chronicled by Michael Black and may well have heightened the sensitivity of what Cambridge curiously calls 'the Central Bodies' to the lesser difficulties experienced by the Examinations Syndicate. The latter did not have to face such acute problems of outdated technology as the Press, but there were signs of staff unrest and deficits on the operating accounts.

In 1970 members of the Syndicate's Assistant Staff went on strike in order to reinforce their demand for higher rates of pay. Frank Wild,

8 Frank Wild, Secretary from 1972 to 1983 (Cambridge Assessment)

Deputy Registrary and former Syndic (1964–7), was sent in as fire-fighter. In early August, he went in person to present a formal report to the Staff at the Syndicate. This was conciliatory in tone, expressing regret that they had not been kept fully informed of the progress of pay negotiations and offering hope of an interim pay rise by September, pending a comprehensive job evaluation. Further action was success-fully discouraged on the grounds that it would not speed up nego-tiations and would only inconvenience the Syndicate Staff and the candidates.

Now regarded as a 'safe pair of hands', Wild was appointed Secre-tary of the Syndicate on the retirement of Brereton's successor, Tom

Wyatt, in 1972. According to a historical survey of the Syndicate's
finances compiled by Michael Halstead in 2000, 'the folklore is that
Dr Wild was sent in to wind the operation up and is reported to
have told the staff that the LES was "broke"'. Although this would
have been an unduly alarmist view of the situation, a loss of around
£180,000, representing some 10–12 per cent of income, was reported
for the financial year ending 31 March 1973. That recovery was so
swift and sustained, notwithstanding the oil crisis of 1974, owed a
great deal to the underlying strength of the operation and Wild's care-
ful husbandry. It was then consolidated by the expansionist policies of
his successor John Reddaway. However, memories of the hard times
undoubtedly coloured the attitude of both men. Nor, indeed, was
their caution misplaced. Overseas business remained precarious, at
the mercy of political decisions beyond the Syndicate's control. It
was not immediately obvious that localisation, where it took place,
would be a long-drawn-out process involving a great deal of consul-
tancy, nor that the organisation would diversify so successfully in the
last decades of the century.

The dependency of the Syndicate on Information Technology (IT)
was a new and increasingly expensive factor in the equation. The first
primitive computer systems had been installed in the 1960s while
the Syndicate was still in its Mill Lane premises, to be succeeded by
ever more sophisticated systems as the technology advanced and business expanded. The 125th Annual Report to the University proudly
announced the installation in 1982 of a new IBM computer which
doubled the Syndicate's previous computing capacity. This gave only
temporary respite. A new and more powerful machine was brought
into service in the winter of 1986, while the network of personal computers and workstations doubled in size in the following two years.
The need to integrate the Syndicate's systems with those of its partners in the Midland Examining Group was a further complication. By
the end of the decade the Syndics decided to move to a bespoke Examinations Processing System (EPS). As many large and complex organisations, including the University, have found to their cost, such systems can easily spiral out of control at the development stage. By 1994,
the project had become bogged down in a morass of revised specifications and was terminated early. It was a hard lesson. Alternative

9 Early examination processing: the punch card room at 1 Mill Lane in the late 1950s or early 1960s (M/P 3/2; photograph by *Cambridge Daily News*)

provision for processing was made and a new system was implemented in stages between 1995 and 1998, but once more the respite was temporary; by 2003, the Syndicate was again looking for a new system.

The issue of Syndicate Staff being subject to University grades and pay scales was not directly addressed at the time of the 1991 review, the committee concluding that 'the present arrangements for staff matters are not unsatisfactory, but should be kept under review'. In effect, the nettle had not been grasped although existing arrangements were creaking at the seams. During the 1970 negotiations with the Assistant Staff, Frank Wild was reported as saying that it could be argued that 'the nature of the Syndicate's work is totally different from that done in other University Departments and hence some autonomy might result'. The fact that the professional Staff of the Syndicate were University Officers and equally tied in with the University's

10 The Data Centre at Cambridge, 2006 (photograph by Nigel Luckhurst)

scale of stipends also caused problems. By the late 1980s the University was in financial straits obliging it to freeze appointments. This was particularly injurious for the Syndicate when GCSE was introduced in the mid 1980s and the Midland Examining Group, of which Cambridge was a part, attracted an unexpectedly large proportion of the candidature. A small number of coursework grades were not processed in time, resulting in delayed results and much excitement in the media. The shortcomings of the Syndicate's computer systems were, in part at least, attributable to the reluctance of highly skilled IT specialists and administrators to be lured by modest academic salaries. The problem diminished, predictably, when the Syndicate was freed from dependence on the University staff structure and was able to offer stipends sufficient to attract the personnel that their burgeoning activities required.

In this respect, comparison with the University Press, a far older institution, is inevitable. Both were, potentially at least, self-sufficient, though both have, at different times, required subventions from, or at least finger-crossing by, the keepers of the University Chest. At no time, however, had it occurred to the University that the technical staff of the Press – compositors, machinists and the like – should be tied into the University staff system, partly at least for historical reasons, as from the earliest years the University printers usually operated as independent traders. The University appointed a printer, later a publisher, later still a Chief Executive, but each of these had a degree of freedom to hire and fire for which the Local Examinations Syndicate was still having to fight. Comparable independence was not achieved until 1995.

PREMISES

The Syndicate did not acquire its own premises until 1885. Initially all the business was managed in the Secretary's rooms. St Catharine's College allotted Browne an extra room, which must have relieved the situation, but the college porters, if no one else, must have been very well aware of the Syndicate as part of the University with the despatch and receipt of examination papers. An application to the Museums and Lecture Room Syndicate for the use of rooms by the Secretary and his clerk was turned down in February 1871, and it was suggested that rooms be found in the town. It was not until 1886 that the Syndicate moved into their first purpose-built premises, designed by W. M. Fawcett, in Mill Lane. The premises comprised a two-storey building with cellars, for 'various purposes'; a ground-floor back room, 36 by 21 feet, chiefly for the preparation of parcels of examination papers, unpacking and sorting answers and so forth; and a ground-floor front room, 18 by 26 feet, for the three permanent clerks (and from one to three temporary clerks). Above were three rooms, a back room for meetings and two front rooms for the secretaries. The whole was described as being 'of a simple domestic character'.

The Syndicate now had a visible presence, adjacent to the Press, to be joined by a separate building, Stuart House, for the Local Lectures staff in 1925, when the Local Lectures were re-launched as the Board of Extra-Mural Studies. The expense of the 1886 building was met from the Syndicate's own funds, and Keynes reported that in

11 Syndicate Buildings, Mill Lane, Cambridge, 1886 (M/P 5/2)

August 1886 he showed his opposite number, Lockhart, Secretary of the Oxford Delegacy for Local Examinations, 'to see over our new buildings, and I fear filled his soul with envy. The University talk of building for him, but the Delegacy have no reserves of their own to fall back upon' – a significant difference in university administration which conspiracy theorists might be tempted to associate with the merger of the Oxford Delegacy and the Syndicate in 1995. Half of one of the two houses belonging to the site purchased in 1885 had been retained as a caretaker's house; this was demolished in 1893 to provide more rooms, and a further extension was mooted in 1938. In the event it was not until 1965 that the Syndicate moved to New Syndicate Buildings on the site of the old Perse School for Boys at 1 Hills Road. This was augmented in 1970 with the opening of the Sir Ivor Jennings Building; in 1985 with that of the Frank Wild Building; in 1998 with that of the Regent Street Building as the Head Office of OCR, by the Chancellor, the Duke of Edinburgh; and, most recently, by that of the 9 Hills Road offices by the Vice-Chancellor in 2005.

12 Syndicate Buildings, 1 Hills Road, Cambridge, on the site of the Perse
School for Boys, 1965 (M/P 5/3; photograph by Henk Snoek)

CONCLUSION

By the 1990s the future looked promising. The Queen's Award for
Export Achievement, granted in 1992, set the seal on the transforma-
tion of the Syndicate to an enterprise prepared for the twenty-first
century. The Press, which received the same award in 1998, was a
similar success story. It might seem that the two organisations would
naturally feed one another: the Examinations Syndicate prescribing
the texts and the Press producing them. This has, indeed, been the
case from time to time, but the potential incestuousness – and it would
surely be seen as such in the world at large – has been skirted, on
either side, doubtless for good reasons. On the other hand, when,
under the leadership of Michael Halstead, the Syndicate disposed

13 1 Regent Street, Cambridge, formerly British Telecom Offices, 2007
(photograph by Nigel Luckhurst)

14 9 Hills Road, Cambridge, formerly S. Cambridgeshire District Council
Offices, 2007 (photograph by Nigel Luckhurst)

15 John Reddaway, Secretary of the Syndicate, receiving the Queen's Award for Export Achievement from James Crowden, Lord Lieutenant of Cambridgeshire, 1992 (M/P 4/2)

of its own presses, the University Press Security Division took on the printing of examination papers. As the University becomes more and more conscious of its overseas commitments and opportunities, it has recognised that both the Press and Cambridge Assessment have overseas offices bearing the Cambridge University banner, of which insufficient use has been made by representatives of the University travelling abroad as they work to attract the academics of the future worldwide. The University now realises that it has not only offices but friends in most, if not all, quarters of the globe, due in no small measure to these two venerable institutions.

2

Cambridge Local Examinations 1858–1945

Andrew Watts

THE FIRST CAMBRIDGE LOCAL EXAMINATIONS

The first students to sit an examination paper set by the University of Cambridge Local Examinations Syndicate did so on 14 December 1858. The examinations took place over the following week in Birmingham, Brighton, Bristol, Cambridge, Grantham, London and Norwich, and they involved 370 students. The cost of running this first year of examinations was just under £424, of which 75 per cent was spent on examiners' fees and expenses, and 20 per cent on printing. The candidates paid an average total fee of just over £1, and the University subsidised the exercise with a contribution of nearly £41, as well as paying the salaries of those administering the Syndicate.

The papers for the examination had no doubt been printed on the new steam presses of Cambridge University Press, a process which enabled more speedy printing than previously. Indeed, the Local Examination system could not have got under way without several technological inventions. One which played a very significant part was the railway, for in those early days examiners appointed in Cambridge travelled to the local centres to 'be responsible for the due conduct of the examination'. Another crucial innovation was the postal service which, as the 'penny post', had been set up in 1838.

EXAMINERS AND LOCAL COMMITTEES

The visiting examiners were helped in their task by local committees. These committees were very significant for the running of the examinations until the early part of the twentieth century and they provided an administrative model that could be easily replicated overseas. The local committee members would often have been teachers, but also included other people interested in improving education, such as the local clergyman. They booked the venue for the examinations, which in many cases would have been a room in a school, and on the day of the examination helped the external examiner to distribute the papers, collect the candidates' answers and return them to Cambridge.

A report on the first year's examination noted that the examiners whose job it was to 'set and look over the papers' had been appointed 'about a month before the time fixed for the examination'. The speed with which the papers were set and printed suggests that the examiners did not, as their modern successors do, have to get their drafts through an extensive process of moderation and checking. But then the examiners were 'university men'. Well into the twentieth century, the tradition of Cambridge University dons marking the Locals' papers remained: apart from anything else it was a useful addition to their salaries. At first they were paid by the difficulty of the subject and the weight of the scripts they marked. In the 1860s, for each pound weight, markers of Arithmetic earned 9 shillings and 6 pence, History 12 shillings, and Classics 18 shillings.

This method of payment led to the ingenious Christmas present from one struggling candidate illustrated on p. 38.

THE SETTING UP OF 'THE SYNDICATE'

The first Annual Report noted that the local committees' assistance was 'always cordially given', their arrangements were 'excellent' and carried out with 'zeal'. 'Zeal' is a word which could be used to describe the whole of the setting up of the local examination system in England. In spring 1857, the University of Cambridge received a deputation from Birmingham and memorials (petitions) from schools in Cheltenham, Leeds and Liverpool requesting that the issue of offering 'local' examinations be considered. In other words, the schools wanted public examinations that students could take without travelling to Cambridge, the expense and trouble of which would have been prohibitive for many of them.

Dear Mr Examiner.

I am sorry I have do such a bad paper but I never did know much Trigonometry. We are all rather excited to day since all the Thero boys have gone home this morning while we have had to stop till now for the exam. So you will be able to understand under what conditions we are doing your exam when you have learnt that we have been here 14 weeks on monday at a stretch and that t we will be in the train in a few hours. I dont don't suppose I must wait to write any more but wishy you a HA MERRY X M A S and PROSPEROUS M NEW YEAR

I remain yours truly

4733

P S. I am sending you a few blank sheets since I believe you are marked paid by weight

16   A letter from candidate 4733, *c.* 1890s (PP/JNK 1/3)

The University's Council of the Senate responded by recommending that a syndicate be set up and this was done on 4 June 1857. The Syndicate reported on 19 November. It proposed that:

– a system of Junior Local Examinations for pupils under fifteen (sixteen was eventually agreed), and Senior Locals for those under eighteen, should be set up;

- the Examinations should cover the following subjects: English Language & Literature, History, Geography, Geology, French, German, Latin, Greek, Chemistry, Physical Sciences, Zoology and Comparative Anatomy, Mathematics, Drawing, Music, Religious Knowledge (unless parents objected);
- the award of 'Associate of Arts' should be made to successful senior candidates, as was proposed at Oxford. This last idea was dropped in Cambridge after intense debate, but it was an interesting idea. The Local Examinations were being set up for 'students not members of the University' – that is, it was assumed that they would end their education after secondary school, and this would be their only chance of being associated with the University.

The University of Cambridge Local Examinations Syndicate was formally set up in February 1858 and the first examinations were held, as we have seen, that December.

TIME AND PLACE

The Syndicate was run at first by one member of the University academic staff (called the Secretary), who recruited others to set and mark the papers. For the first few years the Secretary changed every year. George Forrest Browne, who served from 1870 to 1892, was the first long-term Secretary. He was a Fellow of St Catharine's College and initially ran the Syndicate from his college room. In 1874 he was given, as a concession to his additional duties, a second room in the College. Eventually the Syndicate obtained the funds for the construction of its own building, and in 1886 it moved into 'Syndicate Buildings' in Mill Lane, Cambridge. The Syndicate moved out of this building in 1965 when it moved to its present location at 1 Hills Road.

For the first ninety years the main Cambridge examinations were taken just before Christmas, in a week that came to be known in many countries as 'Cambridge week'. The examinations began on the second or third Monday of December and continued until the following Saturday. In comparison, Oxford's first local examinations were run in the summer of 1858, six months before Cambridge's.

Later Browne wrote, 'We took the only season left open to us by the choice of Oxford.'

This turned out to be an advantage for the Syndicate. When the system was proposed, there were just two terms in the school year, with holidays in the summer and at Christmas. At the same time that the local examinations were getting under way, schools were changing over to a three-term year. Under this system the summer holiday began later, in mid July, and so the Oxford exams were no longer run at the end of the term. The Cambridge examinations, on the other hand, remained just before Christmas and were thus more convenient for three-term schools, an advantage for the Cambridge examinations which was, according to Browne, 'quite unforeseen'.

EXAMINATIONS IN THE AGE OF REFORM

The Local Examinations did not have to be held at the end of the school year because they were not school leaving examinations. Their purpose was to examine the work being done in the schools and to encourage both pupils and teachers to maintain their efforts. In this they were in tune with the spirit of the Victorian age. Under the influence of thinkers like Jeremy Bentham and John Stuart Mill, the idea had taken root that it was the responsibility of society and its members to improve themselves. The engine which would drive this movement would be 'self-help'. As part of a plan for a modern society, Bentham worked out an elaborate examination system for applicants to the Civil Service, and Mill later proposed a system of compulsory education based on an examination system.

In a report written for the fortieth year of the Syndicate it was stated that 'The main object of those who promoted the [local examinations] scheme was to improve the state of education in the schools which lay between the Elementary schools and the great Public [independent] Schools.' The majority of children did not get a chance to go beyond Elementary School, which they would have left by the age of fourteen at the latest. The rapidly expanding middle class expected more from education than that. This section of society was seen to include a range of people, from newly successful industrialists and other profession-als, to clerks and book-keepers, farmers, shop-keepers and tradesmen.

Middle-class schools did not attract government support: they were privately run and parents paid fees, though they may have been supported by endowments. Some of the private secondary schools were good, but in many cases they were poor, so the hope was that they could improve if they had a standard against which to compare themselves.

Various reforming bodies set up systems of examining in the middle of the century. At this time there was a drive towards a more 'modern' curriculum – that is, one which included Science and Modern Languages as well as the Classics (Latin and Greek), which were dominant in the main private schools at the time. In 1853 the Society of Arts (later the Royal Society of Arts) proposed 'a scheme for examining and granting certificates to the class students of (Mechanics) Institutes' which would focus on useful knowledge and practical skills. The Society fairly quickly handed over its examining activity in the Sciences to a government body, the Department of Science and Art, one of whose aims was to encourage schools to take on the teaching of Science, a change which the new examinations supported. From the start the Locals allowed for a practical examination in Chemistry. The detailed list of requirements for this examination, which was sent to the Local Committee, began: 'A separate room should, if possible, be provided for the examination in Practical Chemistry.'

UNIVERSITIES' ROLE IN LOCAL EXAMINATIONS

The local examination system was at first set up by groups of concerned people who together impressed on the universities their responsibility to help raise the standard of education for secondary students. It was a model which was not confined to Oxford and Cambridge. From the 1830s to the early part of the twentieth century, the University of London's entrance, or 'matriculation', examinations were used by some students as the equivalent of a school leaving exam – that is, they took it without any intention of entering the university. After London University was reconstituted by Act of Parliament in 1898, a 'University Extension Board' was specifically given the responsibility of running examinations for secondary schools. The same was true when Victoria University, a federation of colleges in Manchester, Liverpool and Leeds, was set up in the 1880s.

Two people who were involved in the Society of Arts examinations, mentioned above, were Viscount Ebrington and Frederick Temple, and they provide a link with the University of Oxford local examinations. Ebrington was a landowner in Devon, and an MP. He and another local landowner set up their own examination in Exeter at Easter 1856, in which a prize of £20 was offered for the best mark of any young man between eighteen and twenty-three who was the son or relative of a Devon farmer. The Exeter committee asked the Department of Education for help in setting up their examination and they were given Temple, who was a school inspector.

It was Temple who was responsible for setting out a practical scheme of examining which convinced Oxford University that they could run local examinations. His scheme received a warm welcome. The *English Journal of Education* wrote that Temple 'had struck the key to a thousand hearts'. In June 1857 the University of Oxford Delegacy of Local Examinations (UODLE) was established, with the aim of conducting examinations for non-members of the university. At a celebratory meeting in Exeter, Temple stated: 'The universities should be made to feel that they have an interest in the education of all England.'

THE OXFORD DELEGACY AND THE CAMBRIDGE SYNDICATE

It was hoped that eventually the two universities would work together on the delivery of public examinations and in 1860 the suggestion that they should take on the responsibility of running the examinations in alternate years was revived. However, agreement on this could not be reached. At both universities it had been proposed that the title of 'Associate of Arts' was to be awarded to successful senior candidates. Oxford approved this whereas Cambridge did not. This became a cause of disagreement between them, and was the main reason why a jointly run examination system was not established from the start.

From time to time, comparisons were made between the two boards' examinations. In 1872 a headmaster wrote to *The Times* pointing out that the Oxford Locals were attracting fewer candidates than the Cambridge Locals. He suggested reasons for this, including that the Oxford examinations were too hard and they were held in May, as opposed to December which was a 'popular and convenient' time. The headmaster's letter attracted the obvious critical reply that 'A Cambridge certificate is more easily obtained, therefore it is more sought after.' Another writer supported the thesis that Oxford was rightly demanding a higher standard, so Browne wrote to *The Times* to point out that, over the past five years, Cambridge had passed about 7 per cent more juniors than Oxford, and Oxford had passed 7 per cent more seniors. Therefore Cambridge could not be judged to be too lenient. 'I cannot but think', he concluded, 'that your correspondent has taken upon himself a very grave responsibility without due consideration.'

EXAMINATIONS AND GIRLS' EDUCATION

In his autobiography Browne says that when he became Secretary in 1870 the Syndicate was opening the Local Examinations to girls. He was in sympathy with this move, since he had been one of the Cambridge dons who had lectured to women who were taught the material they needed to enter 'unofficially' for the University Tripos examinations. He worked with Miss Clough, the founder of Newnham College, and also with Emily Davies whose students in a house in Hitchin were the forerunners of Girton College. Browne tells how 'a few of us used to go over [to Hitchin] from Cambridge in the afternoon to lecture to them just as we did to the [male] undergraduates in the morning'.

A decision had been taken in 1863 that girls could 'unofficially' sit the examinations in December. This gave the girls in that first year only six weeks to prepare, but the campaigners were determined to make the best of the opportunity. Eighty-three girls took the examinations at the North London Collegiate School run by Miss Frances Mary Buss, who was a campaigner for women's education for most of the second half of the nineteenth century. The next step was a memorial in 1864 to the Cambridge Vice-Chancellor asking that girls should be able to enter the Cambridge Locals officially. It contained nearly 1,000 signatures. A positive report was published in February 1865 and, though the proposal was 'seriously opposed' in the University's Council of the Senate, entry for girls on the same basis as boys was agreed for a three-year period. That year, 126 girls took exams in London, Cambridge, Brighton, Manchester, Bristol and Sheffield. In 1867, eligibility for entry to the Cambridge Locals was made permanent for girls.

In 1868 another memorial was sent to the Vice-Chancellor noting that 'there is not in this country some recognised test of the capacity and attainments of women who desire to become teachers in families or schools'. Therefore in 1869 a Higher Local Examination for women was instituted, for which the age for admission was eighteen. The 'Higher Locals' were opened to men six years later but the number of male candidates was always small. By 1898 there were 1,173 candidates for the Higher Local Examination. In the late nineteenth century this examination was used to award women scholarships to study at Girton and Newnham Colleges in Cambridge, and Bedford College, London. The Syndicate also became formally responsible for the arrangements by which Newnham and Girton students, although still unable to be members of the University, were allowed to take the University degree examinations.

LOCAL LECTURES SYNDICATE

Browne clearly enjoyed lecturing. He enthusiastically took part in the programme of external university lectures which was put on for interested members of the public throughout the country by the University's Local Lectures Syndicate. When it was decided that the two syndicates should merge in 1878 he became the joint Secretary. In the early 1880s he was joined by two Assistant Secretaries, Neville Keynes and James Flather, who were also academic members of the University staff and would eventually become Secretary themselves. The people who looked after the administration of the Syndicate were called 'Clerks', some of whom served the Syndicate for many years. When the two Syndicates were amalgamated there was one permanent Clerk, Mr Crook, and it was decided that another should be appointed. It can be seen what a small operation this was at first, though 'Helpers' were brought in when the volume of work expanded in the examination season.

Both lectures and examinations flourished under Browne. In a valedictory report about him when he left the University in 1892 it was reported that, in 1870, 2,687 candidates had entered for Local Examinations, and 13 schools had been examined. In 1891, these figures had risen to 11,080 and 99, respectively. In the academic year 1877–8, 53 lecture courses had been given, whereas in 1891–2 the number had become about 260. The joint Local Examinations and Lectures Syndicate remained together until 1925 (see above, chapter 1).

EXPANSION OVERSEAS

Very soon after the Local Examinations had started in England, representations were made that they should also be run elsewhere in the world. In December 1862 there was a request from Trinidad 'for some extension of the University action, to schools in the Colonies'. At first the Syndicate thought that 'the difficulties in the way of such an extension were insurmountable' but in 1864 ten candidates sat the Cambridge Locals in Trinidad. This was done 'with the courteous aid of the Colonial Office', encouraged by the Duke of Newcastle, Secretary of State for the Colonies, 'who permitted the examination papers to be sent in sealed parcels to the Governor'. In 1869 a similar request came from HM Inspector of Schools for South Africa in Natal and it was agreed to extend the Syndicate's examinations there the following year. Further applications were received from Royal College, Mauritius (in 1873), from Wellington, New Zealand and Georgetown, Demerara – now part of Guyana – (1874), and from the Straits Settlements in Malaya (1891). In Jamaica the Junior Locals were first held in 1882 and the Higher Locals ten years later.

A report on the 1892 examinations in Ceylon noted that there were nearly as many candidates there as in the other overseas countries put together, with centres in Colombo, Kandy, Galle and Jaffna. The candidates there obtained a good number of distinctions and a student called L. A. E. de Zilwa, of St Thomas's College, gained the English University Scholarship, worth £150, tenable for four years. The same report noted that another scholar, S. W. Dassenaike, who was studying

LOCAL EXAMINATIONS AND LECTURES SYNDICATE

SCHOOL CERTIFICATE

This is to certify that

George Lygo

having pursued a course of study for at least three years at the following Approved School

Grammar School Burton on Trent

in the subjects stated on the back of this Certificate has passed the

Senior Local Examination

reaching the required standard in Group I English Subjects Group II Languages other than English Group III Mathematics and Science and has passed with credit in *ten* subjects namely

1 Religious Knowledge 2 English Literature
3 English History 4 Geography 5 Latin
6 French and Spoken French
7 Arithmetic Geometry Algebra 8 Trigonometry
9 Heat Electricity & Magnetism Practical Physics
10 Natural History

The student was placed in the *Second* Class of Honours

Age *14* Date of Examination *July 1919*

Index-number *332* Centre *Burton on Trent*

P. Giles.
Vice-Chancellor

The Board of Education have inspected the School and recognised it as an efficient Secondary School and accept the Examination as reaching the approved standard and as being suitable for the School

Signed on behalf of
the Board of Education

W. N. Bruce Assistant Secretary

17 Certificate for the Senior Local Examination, 1919. Note that it was issued by the Local Examinations and Lectures Syndicate and bore the Vice-Chancellor's signature (A/C 2/2)

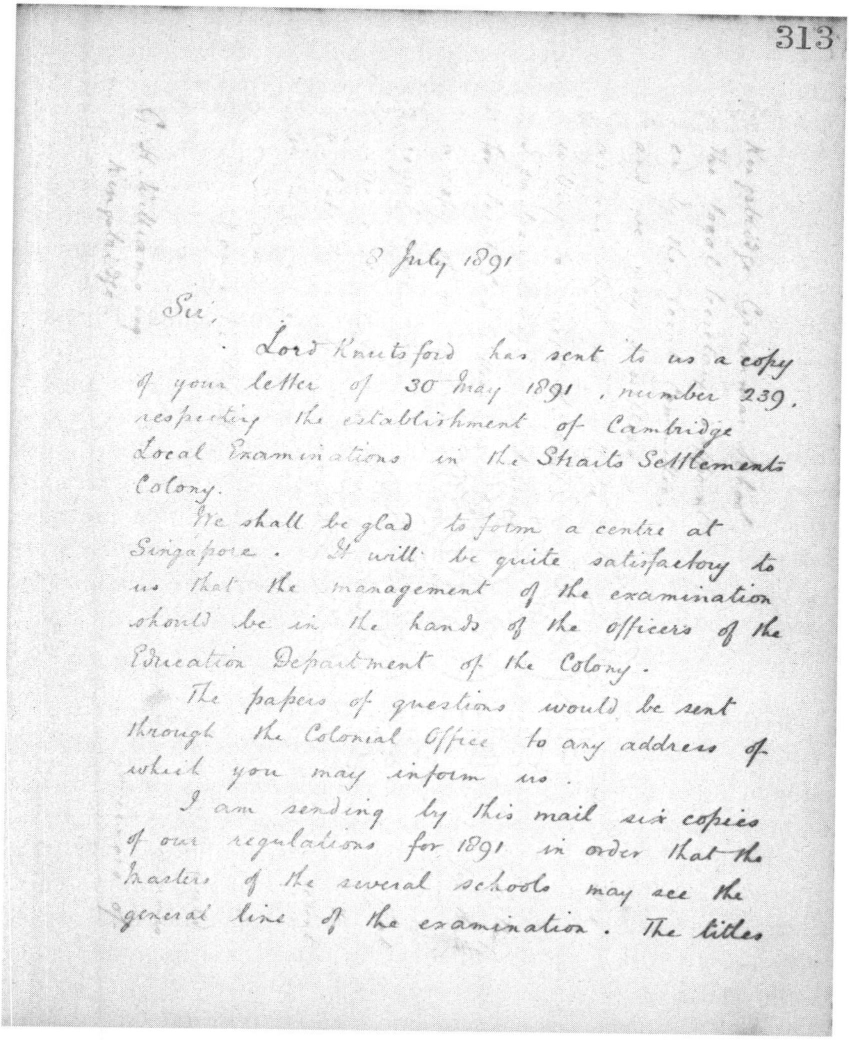

313

8 July 1891

Sir,

Lord Knutsford has sent to us a copy
of your letter of 30 May 1891, number 239,
respecting the establishment of Cambridge
Local Examinations in the Straits Settlements
Colony.

We shall be glad to form a centre at
Singapore. It will be quite satisfactory to
us that the management of the examination
should be in the hands of the officers of the
Education Department of the Colony.

The papers of questions would be sent
through the Colonial Office to any address of
which you may inform us.

I am sending by this mail six copies
of our regulations for 1891 in order that the
masters of the several schools may see the
general line of the examination. The titles

18 Letter of 8 July 1891 concerning the establishment of Cambridge
examinations in the Straits Settlements (A/LB 1/2)

Engineering at the Royal Indian Engineering College, Cooper's Hill, was 'maintaining the prestige of the Island youth for capacity and industry. In the first year's examination he came out head of the class of students for that year.'

The expected difficulties in running international examinations certainly did present a challenge. In 1875 the papers for December had to be set by Easter, so that they could be printed and despatched to the colonies in September and early October. In 1897 the papers from the Gold Coast (Ghana) did not arrive back in Cambridge because both the Acting Director of Education and the Acting Colonial Chaplain had died and no-one knew where they had put the candidates' completed scripts. Eventually, a 'key put away among a heap of papers' was found which could open a box in which the missing papers were stored. In 1898, in Mauritius, 'Cambridge week' had to be postponed from 17 December to 27 December, because the steamer carrying the papers had been delayed. This gave rise to the claim that the delay had enabled two papers to be cabled to a candidate in Mauritius, from a centre which had already taken the examination, a charge which the Syndicate dismissed as 'wildly improbable'.

CREATION OF THE OXFORD AND CAMBRIDGE BOARD

Opponents of the Locals had always had reservations about the fact that they encouraged the examining of individuals, not whole classes or schools. This was a widely held view in the public schools (that is, private schools in England), along with fear of state interference. These schools argued for a combined system of examining and inspection, but one which was administered by the ancient universities not the government.

In 1871 a request was made to Oxford and Cambridge Universities to set up a system to examine 'first-grade' schools and individual students of sixteen and nineteen studying there. Thus the Oxford and Cambridge Schools Examination Board (OCSEB) was created in 1873, partly to preserve the public schools from 'the centralizing uniformity or the arbitrary caprice of a government department'. This development was mainly seen as extending to the public schools what had already been done for middle-class schools, but OCSEB went further in the linking of schools to the universities. The Board offered a 'Higher Certificate' examination three times a year, and internal examinations could also be requested and individually prepared by the Board at any time.

EXAMINATION AND INSPECTION

People who believed that the focus should be more on groups of children and schools than on individual pupils argued for a combination of examinations and inspections. The Syndicate offered such a service to schools, beginning with a decision in 1862 in which it was agreed that the examination of schools should be a part of the University extension programme. Under this scheme, the term 'to examine schools' meant to set examinations, to inspect the schools and also in some cases to certify the teachers. Cambridge colleges appointed inspectors and, in 1864, four schools were examined in this way.

The arrangements for the inspections were that examiners were appointed by the Syndicate and the school than drew up a programme for their visit. During this, the examiners observed classes being taught, conducted oral examinations of classes, or set some examination papers for the students to do. These were marked either by themselves or, initially, by the school staff. Examiners could visit schools annually and the Syndicate's policy was to send the same examiner for up to three years to gain the benefits of continuity. Schools could publish the reports of the examiners but, if they did, the whole report had to be made public. The Syndicate favoured a combination of inspection and local examinations for pupils able to do them, and thus did not advocate that every student took an examination. At the fortieth anniversary of the Syndicate, inspection was still important either in conjunction with the local examinations or independently of them. In that year, 1898, independently of the local examinations, 124 schools containing approximately 16,000 pupils were inspected and examined by the Syndicate.

Table 1

Year		Centres	Juniors	Seniors
1858	Boys	8	297	73
1878	Boys	93	3329	626
	Girls	81	1483	997
1898	Boys	244	5516	801
	Girls	213	2954	1414

CHALLENGES TO EXAMINATIONS

The figures in table 1 show the steady growth of the Cambridge home examinations in the first forty years of their existence. There was satisfaction within the Syndicate with the progress that was being made. However, we have seen above that there were reservations about the examination system from the start and, as it became embedded, concerns were expressed with increasing frequency.

One of the earliest criticisms of the Locals was that the achievements of a few were purchased at the expense of the many. This was because in some classes only a few children were deemed able enough to take the examinations, but the curriculum of the whole class was geared to their needs. Cramming and too much competition were also claimed to be causing pupils to become over-strained. Complaints such as the following surfaced regularly in the reports of examiners to the Syndicate: 'The examiners regret to notice the prevalence of the bad habit of making the children learn by rote concise notes from text books, without making sure that they understand what is meant.' Concerning the Junior Shakespeare paper in December 1893 an examiner wrote: 'the candidates are crammed at most centres with such desperate cunning that the innocent amateur [here referring to the newly appointed examiner] at the work of setting his first papers is tolerably sure to find himself scored off. There is an absolute necessity of making the bulk of the paper involve genuine knowledge of the text of the plays.' The students were not blamed for this, though, and a humane tone is sometimes to be heard. In writing about a Dictation paper in the same year, one examiner commented, 'the greatest difficulty was found in "Alexander", for

CAMBRIDGE HIGHER LOCALS.

To the Editor of The Journal of Education.

SIR,—I shall be glad if you will allow me to make a few remarks on the examination in English Literature in the Cambridge Higher Local for 1893.

The syllabus is as follows :

" 2. History of English Literature.

"The examination will be on the period from 1688 to 1760. Special value will be attached to first-hand acquaintance with the principal works (published during the given period) of Dryden, Addison, Pope, Thomson, Johnson, and Gray."

The paper, so far from encouraging " first-hand acquaintance " with the authors mentioned, scarcely gives a chance to the candidate of showing that he has read them. There are twelve questions, of which four of the first half and four of the second may be answered. The first half can be answered only by " cramming " some book on English literature. The first four questions do not allude to the authors named in the syllabus ; the fifth and sixth are only the commonplaces of the text-books with regard to Addison and Swift, the latter not being an author recommended for reading. There is a question about the political and philosophical teaching of John Locke, also not named, and a question about the development of fiction during the reign of George II., which, of course, could be best answered by a first-hand acquaintance with Smollett and Fielding. Do the examiners deliberately wish to encourage such acquaintance ? Other names—Berkeley, Bishop Butler, Mandeville, Parnell, Pepys, Shenstone—are asked about ; but, of course, only second-hand acquaintance with them is asked for.

Let us turn to the second half of the paper.

" 7. Mention any works of permanent value published by Dryden after the Revolution, and *summarize their character and contents.* How was he personally affected by the political changes ? Indicate his position as linking two distinct periods in literature."

19 Cutting from the *Journal of Education* 1893 criticising the English Literature paper in the Higher Local Examination for that year (PP/JNK 2/2)

which word youthful ingenuity contrived to find nearly forty different spellings'.

Whether the examinations were too hard even for 'average pupils' was also a topic of debate and school teachers often made the point that the wrong people were doing the examining. The *Journal of Education*, for example, accepted that the examinations had played a part in giving proof of efficient teaching, but objected that teachers had 'so little to say as regards the method of examining'. The examinations, the *Journal* claimed, were 'ruled and regulated by middle-aged and even elderly gentlemen, who now have little to do with the education of the young, and in many cases have never had to do with it'.

The first serious statistical studies of examination results were undertaken in 1888–90 by F. Y. Edgeworth, an economist at Oxford. He applied the theory of error in measurement to examinations and referred to the 'unavoidable uncertainty' of the results. Edgeworth supported the use of public examinations and described their purpose as a 'species of sortition' for scholarships, university places and appointments to the Civil Service. The problem with them was the unreliability of their results. He described them as 'a sort of lottery in which the chances are better for the more deserving'. He therefore proposed that the boards, when they published the results, should grade candidates (as at Oxford) rather than rank them, as Cambridge did, in order not to claim greater exactitude than was believable. The easy confidence of the early years of examining – that the examiners would quickly distinguish which candidate was better than another – had not been borne out in practice.

PRELIMINARY EXAMINATIONS

It was also clear that there were deeper inequalities in the system, as open competition gave a premium to those who had obtained the best early education. It was painfully obvious, from the high failure rate in the early preliminary examinations of the Locals, that many students were unable to get over the hurdle of attaining a standard of literacy and numeracy that would enable them to tackle the local examinations effectively.

In 1895 the Syndicate started to offer a Preliminary Local Examination for students of fourteen and under in the lower forms of secondary schools, some of whom might leave to take up a job before they took the Junior Locals. This examination proved popular, and in 1898 5,256 candidates entered. The innovation was not welcomed by all, however. The *Journal of Education* in January 1895 complained that 'a competitive examination for boys and girls of thirteen or under is absolutely indefensible on physiological grounds . . . [it also] encourages masters and mistresses to teach not the subjects that are the best gymnastic for their pupils but those which will obtain, at least cost, the greatest number of distinctions for their schools'. Many teachers felt that it was the responsibility of the school heads and their staff to examine their own young pupils, and they should not be subjected to another public examination.

THE BRYCE COMMISSION

In 1894 a Royal Commission on Secondary Education in England was set up, under the chairmanship of James Bryce. This Commission's work laid down the pattern according to which education in England and Wales was to be organised in the next century. It recommended that a central government board should 'supervise the Secondary Education of the country' with a government minister overseeing it. It also proposed the setting up of Local Authorities to ensure the provision of education in the counties and county boroughs. Following these recommendations a Board of Education was set up in 1899 and the so-called 'Balfour Education Act' in 1902 laid down that Local Education Authorities should be established.

By this time the Secretary of the Syndicate was Neville Keynes, who had been appointed in 1892, having been Assistant Secretary under Browne for the previous eleven years. Keynes presented the Syndicate's views to the Bryce Commission in a memorandum in June 1894. He referred to the original aim of the Local Examinations to improve the state of education in secondary schools and he claimed:

The high character of the work sent in by the pupils at many of the schools which regularly prepare candidates, and the gradual rise which has on the whole taken place in the difficulty of the examinations, afford a satisfactory evidence of progress. The Syndicate believe that this progress may fairly be attributed in a considerable degree to the local examinations themselves.

Mindful of criticisms which had been aimed at the Syndicate, Keynes pointed out that 'a considerable proportion of the examiners . . . have been actual teachers in schools, or are in direct and continuous contact with school work by means of the examination and personal inspection of individual schools which they undertake on behalf of the Syndicate'. Another criticism to which he alluded was the ill-effect of imposing the examinations on all pupils. Keynes suggested that 'A system which often works well is a combination of a school inspection with the local examinations, the higher forms alone taking the latter, while the lower forms are inspected and examined separately.' The aim was 'to give as free a scope as possible to the development of schools' with each school at liberty 'to develop its work according to its own ideal'. It was, as Keynes said, an 'extremely elastic' system, and he concluded that 'A varied system is best adapted to the circumstances in England.'

The arguments against excessive central control had their effect. The Commission had set out 'to guard against excessive multiplication and overlapping of examinations' but, bearing in mind the various needs of the different classes of schools, it did not conclude that the examinations should be run by a 'Central Authority'. It recommended that the Board of Education should frame regulations for the examining bodies which should be recognised as competent or suitable to conduct the examinations of such schools. There would be an 'Educational Council', four of whose members would be appointed by the Universities of Oxford, Cambridge, London and Victoria (Manchester). One of the duties of the Educational Council would be to advise the Minister concerning 'regulations for the inspection and the conduct of examinations'. However, the Minister would have the power to overrule the Council. The proposals, for the time being, left the examinations in the hands of the universities, and in November 1896 a memorial was sent from Cambridge University to the government, welcoming the proposals of the Bryce Commission. It was high time that secondary education in England was properly organised, and the University wished to 'urge upon the government the importance of introducing legislation upon the subject'.

FORTIETH ANNIVERSARY AND THE PARIS EXHIBITION

A pamphlet produced for the Syndicate's fortieth anniversary noted that 'in its fundamental character the scheme now in operation is identical with that which was initiated in 1858'. As it approached the new century, the Syndicate was confident that the system of local examinations had indeed led to the kinds of improvements which had

Table 2

	Preliminary boys	Preliminary girls	Junior boys	Junior girls	Senior Boys	Senior Girls	Total
1898	3173	2083	5516	2954	801	1414	15941
1907	2814	1959	5334	3381	2463	2962	18913

been desired at the outset. The pamphlet pointed out that holders of Higher and Senior Local Examination certificates could be exempted from the 'Previous (or preliminary) Examinations' of the University and that they therefore functioned as a school leaving exam. Holders of these certificates could also be exempted from the preliminary examinations of professional bodies such as the Law Society, the General Medical Council and the Royal Institute of British Architects.

During 1899, there was some discussion about what sort of contribution the Syndicate should make to the coming 1900 Paris Exhibition to celebrate the turn of the century. It was decided that the Syndicate would, as part of a Cambridge 'English Education' exhibition, 'contribute exhibits, illustrative of the work of the Local Examinations, together with worked papers'. Eventually it was decided not to send papers written by students, but to send 'copies of examination papers and reports, forms of certificates, statistics etc.'. The anniversary leaflet mentioned above was also translated into French. The exhibits sent to Paris are still held in the Cambridge Assessment Archive: they comprise a map of the UK and of the world showing the location of centres, and also graphs showing the increase in numbers of candidates over the forty years of the Syndicate's existence.

During the next ten years the pattern of entries for the Cambridge Locals would show some of the changes that were taking place in education in England (Table 2 above). Overall, the numbers of candidates increased, and this was mainly accounted for by the increased numbers for the senior examinations. The numbers of boys and girls taking the preliminaries and of boys taking the juniors dropped slightly, indicating that there was a tendency for students to continue further into secondary education. The Cambridge Syndicate's strong link with examinations for girls can also be seen in these figures.

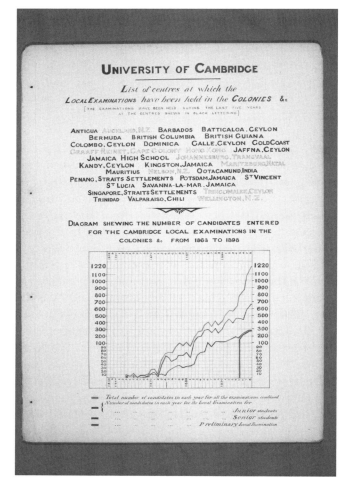

20 A board from the exhibition sent to Paris in 1900 showing the growth of
colonial examinations (M/PE 1; photograph by Nigel Luckhurst)

OVERSEAS EXPANSION FOR THE SYNDICATE

In his memorandum to the Bryce Commission, Keynes wrote that
in 1893 there were twelve centres 'in the colonies, the total number
of colonial candidates being 570'. By the fortieth anniversary in 1898
this had risen to 1,220 candidates from thirty-six centres. Keynes

noted in his memo that colonial schools valued the opportunity to compare their results with those of schools in England. The Local Examinations were by then also being used to offer scholarships to enable boys to take up places at boarding school or university in England. Over the next twenty years, Cambridge examinations were used to award scholarships such as the Barbados Scholarship, the Jamaica Scholarship and the Queen's Scholarships of Malaya, all tenable at British universities. Scholarships for Girton College and Newnham were similarly awarded to girls.

There was close co-operation between the Syndicate and the Colonial Administration. In 1898 the Governor of Mauritius, Sir Charles Bruce, wrote that he had introduced the system of local examinations to Ceylon and Mauritius, and had done his 'best to encourage [it] in the West Indies'. In Ceylon the Syndicate discussed with the Director of Public Instruction whether Tamil and Sinhalese should be examined. The Director was in favour, as it 'would undoubtedly be a great help towards the solution of educational difficulties here'.

It is true that initially the candidates were mostly children of the European administrators, but after 1900 a study of the names of candidates who passed in the Cambridge exams shows that local candidates were beginning to take advantage of the opportunities offered. Some of these students joined the colonial administrative service or commercial concerns and were to become a significant force in their countries. In the Federated Malay States, from 1921, applicants for a probationership in the Malay Administration Service were required to hold a Cambridge Junior Certificate, and in 1930 this requirement was raised to a Senior Certificate. During the period 1919 to 1938 the number of holders of the Cambridge Senior Certificate there rose from 47 to 671.

The examination of local languages was the first area in which a more international curriculum was recognised. In 1910, Arabic and Sanskrit were added to the Senior Locals, and Chinese, in response to a request from the Shanghai centre. In 1918, Tamil and Sinhalese were both included in the Junior and Senior examinations for Ceylon. In 1919, Hindi and Urdu were made available for senior students, and the next year junior and senior syllabuses in Malay were approved. The examiners for these subjects, who had to be resident in the

UK, were mainly found with advice from the School of Oriental and African Studies (which was founded in 1917 and given its present name in 1938).

Other attempts were also made to provide more familiar contexts in the overseas papers for candidates from overseas centres, and also to prepare them for the working life they would soon enter. A report on the Junior Book-Keeping and Commercial Arithmetic Examinations (for 18-year-olds) in 1899 noted that 'very few candidates were able to explain the effect of a fall in the exchange value of the rupee on the business of a merchant in India'. However, the inclusion of other subjects appeared more problematic and people in other countries must have questioned the Syndicate's apparent reluctance to make the curriculum less Anglo-centric. In 1907 a request was made from the local Darjeeling girls' secretary to include Indian History as one of the subjects to be studied, but this did not appear in the School Certificate regulations until 1931.

FIRST WORLD WAR

The work overseas was obviously going to be disrupted at the outbreak of war in 1914. The first evidence of this in October of that year was a spate of resignations as men left the staff to join the army, and their posts were left open or filled by temporary clerks. During the December examinations, enemy shells fell on Hartlepool, Scarborough and Whitby and disrupted an Arithmetic examination. A special paper was sent to the three centres and the students sat it later the same week. The Assistant Secretary, Nalder Williams, who after the war became Secretary, was called up and the military appealed against an attempt to exempt him. Only a petition, signed by the Syndics and stating the value of the work he was doing, enabled him to stay in Cambridge. (As late as the 1980s, the memories of those years still rankled in Jack Roach's description of Williams as: 'a Syndic during the First War, asked to do the job when people were in short supply, he not having gone off to serve'.)

The Syndicate's centres were generally not in areas affected by the war, though in 1915 scripts from West Africa were lost when the SS *Appam* was captured. For the 1917 examinations the Syndicate continued to do what it could to support the war effort: 'In view of the importance of economy in paper in the present circumstances the Syndicate have decided to follow the course which they have adopted for the last two years, and not to publish the examiners' reports.' Over the four-year period of the war, candidature fell by nearly 11 per cent, from 24,011 to 22,371. However, the war was not totally disruptive: in the July of 1918 nearly 1,000 students took Cambridge examinations from colonial centres, and in December, nearly 600. The difficulties of the war were mentioned in the Annual Report, especially those affecting colonial centres. It was reported that 'the candidates' answers have all been safely conveyed from the centres to Cambridge, except a small number of Higher Local answers which were on a ship torpedoed off the Indian coast in June 1917'. Just as was to be the case in the Second World War, it seemed that those involved with the examinations were, as far as possible, determined to carry on with life as usual.

Other notable issues came before the Syndicate during the war, which hint at the wider reality. In contrast to its previous refusal to appoint women as presiding examiners for the Higher Local Examinations, in May 1916 and April 1918, respectively, female presiding examiners were appointed in two centres, as 'no male graduate was available'. In March 1917, the Syndicate agreed to send a representative to a conference at the Board of Education concerning British prisoners of war in Ruhleben. It was also agreed that there should be no distinction between military and civilian prisoners. Finally, two days after the Armistice was signed, it was decided that the war bonus should continue to be paid to clerks 'until there was some fall in prices'.

INVOLVEMENT OF TEACHERS

In January 1916 the Board of Education sent a request to the Syndicate that 'some provision may be made for bringing teachers more definitely in touch with the examinations'. Over two years later and a fortnight before the Armistice was signed, a Joint Committee for Examinations, which included both male and female teachers, first met. The Chairman, the President of Queens' College, opened the meeting by telling the committee that 'We are here to work, not talk'! The topics discussed included some difficulties in the proposed timetabling of the Senior Locals; specific proposals about Science, Art, Physics, and Experimental Science syllabuses; and 'the undue strain imposed on a child's judgement by having to choose one out of several subjects' for the English Composition. The concerns of teachers were at last being officially noted.

A later Secretary, Joseph Brereton, wrote in 1944 that UCLES was slow to bring teachers into its councils. He believed that the success of the Northern Universities Joint Matriculation Board in its first thirty years of existence was 'traceable to the presence on it of teachers actually working in the schools taking the examinations'. Brereton felt that it was only in 1932 that Cambridge began to profit similarly when it included as members of the Syndicate three principals of schools and one Director of Education.

THE SCHOOL CERTIFICATE REPLACES THE SENIOR LOCALS

In 1911 the Board of Education had proposed that a School Certificate Examination system should be set up, but this process stalled during the First World War and it was not until 1918 that the first School Certificate Examinations were held. The latter was also the first year for the Higher School Certificate. It was, as envisaged by the Bryce Commission, a national system, with the Board of Education, through a Secondary School Examinations Council (set up in 1917), being the co-ordinating authority. The system was designed to produce evidence of general educational attainment which could replace the qualifying examinations of the different providers, including the universities' own matriculation examinations. The examinations were still to be set and marked, and the certificates awarded, by the university boards, which were therefore referred to as 'awarding bodies'. By this time these included the Joint Matriculation Board, set up in 1903 and run by Manchester, Liverpool, Sheffield, Leeds and Birmingham universities.

Both the School Certificate (SC) and Higher School Certificate (HSC) were 'group' examinations. To obtain a School Certificate the student had to reach the required standard in five subjects, with at least one of the subjects being chosen from a selection of Humanities, Languages and Maths/Science. By 1950, this requirement had been adapted to five subjects which must include English, a language and Maths/Science. For HSC, the students at first had to take three main subjects and one subsidiary, a regulation that was later modified to two principal and two subsidiary, or three main, subjects.

The School Certificate system was the first, unified secondary school examination system for the country and it considerably simplified the situation for schools and students. The standard of the new Higher School Certificate Examinations was linked to the Higher Locals and its use made the taking of university matriculation examination unnecessary. The arrangements brought into effect for the HSC thus foreshadowed the introduction of A levels thirty-three years later. It is of interest to note that the debit side of the new group SC and HSC awards was soon being commented on: it was, for example, noted that, in 1932, 30 per cent of the candidates who failed the School Certificate Examinations did so because of only one subject. It was this kind of evidence which led to the abandonment of group examinations when the General Certificate of Education system was introduced in the 1950s.

INTERNATIONAL DEVELOPMENTS

During the 1920s and 1930s, the examination system was changing at home and the issue therefore arose of how far the examinations for other countries should also change. The Preliminary Exam was discontinued in 1920 in England, though it continued to be used overseas until 1939. The Junior Locals, which ended in England in 1939, continued until 1953 internationally. Also, in 1923, the newly introduced School and Higher School Certificates replaced the Senior Locals and Higher Locals in England, and again this raised the issue of whether these changes should also be implemented internationally.

In addition, the policy of the British government began to change in favour of reflecting the different circumstances of the different colonies. In 1924 the Secretary of State for the Colonies set up an Advisory Committee on Education in the African dependencies, which stated that 'Education should be adapted to the mentality, aptitudes, occupations and traditions of the various peoples.' In 1928, W. G. A. Ormsby-Gore, a Parliamentary Under-Secretary, visited Malaya and Ceylon and reported the 'distorting and harmful effects' of external examinations on their education systems. In discussions within the Colonial Office it was, however, acknowledged that external examinations set an international standard, and that this link was of benefit to the local students. Such qualifications were readily recognised by British universities and professional bodies. In 1929 the Advisory Committee on Education in the Colonies recommended that examining bodies and colonial authorities should 'explore the possibilities not only of local examinations, but also of external examinations adapted in syllabus to local conditions, and employing as often as possible local examiners'.

The Syndicate responded by setting up, in November 1933, a Joint Committee for Oversea Examinations. A representative of the government Advisory Committee on Education in the Colonies sat on this, and also nominees of the Directors of Education in Ceylon, Malaya and India. The Syndicate also set up two schemes in Nigeria which allowed for locally devised syllabuses and the local setting and marking of examination papers. Similarly, in Malaya a special examination in English Literature was set up in 1930, with a syllabus devised in Malaya and marked there, with the marking revised in England.

Although Oxford's Locals and London's Matriculation examinations were also exported, the Cambridge Syndicate was the most prominent British body awarding school leaving certificates overseas. In 1934 the London Board proposed to open an examination centre in British Guiana (Guyana) for secondary students. London's Matriculation examinations were already well known as an entry qualification for its external degrees, so this competition at the secondary level alarmed the Syndicate. In 1936, therefore, the Colonial Office set up a Joint Advisory Board, in which the principle for the provision of school leaving examinations of 'one dependency, one examining board' was agreed.

Clearly, the provision of new forms of examination for the colonies was an issue which linked to larger issues of self-determination and independence for those countries. The progress towards taking control of their own education systems must have seemed slow, and this was reflected in the wider disappointment voiced about the conservative provisions of the Colonial Development Act in 1929, which were limited and unsympathetic to non-European aspirations. It could be argued that the examinations were an aspect of cultural imperialism. The examination systems which had grown up in the overseas dependencies appeared to place constraints on local secondary education, emphasising the learning of the English language and familiarity with English culture, and tending to favour a small class of selected students. On the other hand, as has been pointed out by Ali Mazrui, a European education gave renewed status to literacy and knowledge, which opened the door for local people to obtain new opportunities for influence. Those holding Cambridge certificates could find work in the government service and would eventually play their part in running their own countries after independence.

THE MEASUREMENT OF HUMAN ABILITY

By the early twentieth century, following the work of scholars like Edgeworth, the element of chance in written examinations had been recognised. Others, like Francis Galton in the UK, Alfred Binet in France and John Cattell in the USA, were developing the new science of psychometrics, working on the idea that it was possible to measure human abilities and achievement scientifically. Cattell reasonably pointed out that 'when students are excluded from college because they do not secure a certain grade in a written examination, or when candidates for positions in the government service are selected as a result of written examinations . . . the least we can do is to make a scientific study of our methods and results'.

In the 1920s and 1930s in the UK, Cyril Burt, a psychologist for the education department of the London County Council, championed the use of more objective intelligence tests, and these were eventually used after the Second World War for selection to secondary schools in England and Wales. In 1932, C. W. Valentine (Professor of Education at Birmingham University) and W. G. Emmet published *The Reliability of Examinations: an Enquiry*. Sir Philip Hartog and

16   EXAMINATION PAPERS (JUNIOR)

English History

(One hour and a half)

[*Candidates should answer* **five,** *but* **not more than five,** *of the following thirty-two questions. The questions may be taken from* **one** *or* **two,** *but* **not more,** *of the four periods* **A, B, C, D.**]

A. 1066—1485.

1. What was done by William I and Lanfranc for the Church in England?

2. Show how Henry II restored order in England.

3. Why did the Barons make King John accept Magna Carta?

4. Give a brief account of Edward I's dealings with **either** Scotland **or** Wales.

5. Write a brief account of Edward III's war with France down to the Treaty of Bretigny (1360).

6. Write a brief description of a medieval village and the life of the villagers.

7. Give an account of the career of Warwick 'the King-Maker.'

8. Write notes on **three** of the following: (*a*) Anselm; (*b*) Hubert Walter; (*c*) Simon de Montfort; (*d*) the Black Death; (*e*) Caxton.

B. 1485—1688.

9. What great changes first began to show themselves in the reign of Henry VII?

10. Give an account of the work of the Reformation Parliament, 1529–1536.

11. What were Mary's objects at her accession? How far did she succeed in them?

12. Why did Philip II of Spain send the Armada against England? Describe its defeat.

21 English History paper for overseas candidates for the Junior Examination, December 1940 (Bound Volume 1940)

13. Give an account of the eleven years 'Tyranny', 1629–1640.

14. Why was Charles II brought back in 1660? What else was then restored besides the monarchy?

15. Trace the steps leading to the downfall of James II.

16. Write notes on **three** of the following: (*a*) the Field of Cloth of Gold; (*b*) Sir Walter Raleigh; (*c*) the Pilgrim Fathers; (*d*) the Solemn League and Covenant; (*e*) the Clarendon Code.

C. 1688—1815.

17. How did William III deal with Ireland?

18. Give an account of the career of Marlborough.

19. Show the importance of the following in Walpole's career: (*a*) the South Sea Bubble; (*b*) Queen Caroline; (*c*) the Excise Bill: (*d*) the War of Jenkins's Ear.

20. Describe briefly of the career and importance of the Elder Pitt.

21. Against what opponents had Britain to fight in the War of American Independence? What did she lose by the War?

22. How was English farming altered in the 18th century? To whom were the various changes mainly due?

23. What part did the British Army play in the overthrow of Napoleon?

24. Write notes on **three** of the following: (*a*) the battle of Killiecrankie; (*b*) the Pragmatic Sanction; (*c*) the siege of Arcot; (*d*) James Watt; (*e*) the Act of Union, 1800.

D. 1815—1914.

25. Give an account of the distress which marked the years 1815–1822.

26. What were the chief reforms carried out by Sir Robert Peel?

2

E. C. Rhodes also wrote *An Examination of Examinations* in 1935 in which the systems used by the examination boards in the School Certificate were criticised. This work was based on the researches of a committee which tried to test experimentally the reliability of markers' marking. Hartog claimed that there had been no systematic investigation by the boards that the marks awarded by their examiners were consistent – indeed his studies produced evidence that they were not. In some cases, and a School Certificate paper in History from one of the boards was given as a striking example, the Hartog Committee claimed that 'the irregularities may be so large as entirely to discredit the value of the test'.

However, in spite of some support for more objectivity in achievement testing, traditional examining continued in England. The Cambridge papers continued to emphasise curriculum, required essay-length answers, and relied on subjective judgements by examiners. In response to Hartog's criticisms, Jack Roach, an Assistant Secretary at the Syndicate, explained the Syndicate's way of dealing with these things. Mark schemes were discussed by examiners, sample papers were exchanged, meetings held, and the examiners were under constant supervision from a Chief Examiner. The aim was to 'impose the standard of the Chief Examiners on their marking teams'; consistency in marking meant being in tune with his standards. In addition, scaling was used to balance different parts of the examination and unfairness was avoided by 'giving the fullest consideration to each individual'. If a student had one paper out of line with the others, it was rechecked and remarked if necessary.

In 1944 Joseph Brereton, the other Assistant Secretary at the time, published a book entitled *The Case for Examinations*, which sought to answer the critics of the system. He addressed the issues raised by what he described as 'the attempt to reduce examinations to mere measuring devices'. His main point was that examinations were a 'mobilising force in education', and their purpose was to stimulate teachers and students. They were thus intimately linked to the courses of study leading to them and in this respect they differed from intelligence and aptitude tests. The latter 'have no concern with a previous course of preparation, and in fact presuppose that there has been no such

22 Standard setting for the Sudan, 1955 (M/P 1/4; photograph by Ramsey and Muspratt Studios, Cambridge)

course'. Writing in 1965, in another book *Exams: Where Next?*, he reiterated his view:

I find that my method of judging different types of examination questions is different from that of many critics. I instinctively look beyond the question itself to the activity or learning process which it is examining. Others tend to keep in mind the knowledge or skill supposed to be tested, while I think about what the student and his teachers are likely to do in order to prepare for such questions.

THE SYNDICATE'S PLACE IN WORLD EDUCATION

The roles of a curriculum and examination system originating in some British universities had been questioned in the years between the two world wars. With the advent of the Certificate of Proficiency in English (CPE) in 1913 (see chapter 5), the Syndicate had begun to address both the cultural place of the work it was encouraging and its practical use. Jack Roach, who worked to build up the CPE, particularly in Europe, was a linguist who had a strong view of the outcomes he desired. In a paper in 1935 entitled 'Modern Languages and International Relations' he wrote 'a modern language course is not only a mental discipline: it is a preparation for life'. He had fought in the First World War and counted himself among those of his generation who 'share in the growing desire to "put things right"'.

In a later paper Roach noted with approval a report on secondary education which 'defined one object of modern language teaching as the "enlargement of sympathy"'. As the Second World War began, he feared 'an outbreak of British insularity which would unfit us still further to lead Europe along the paths of peaceful cooperation'. Political exploitation of such a sentiment might 'deflect the British people from a generous and genuinely international pursuit of war aims'. Roach's attitudes were those of the Syndicate after the war. In a paper entitled 'Policy and Future Development', written as the war was coming to an end, he envisaged what would be the chosen path: 'the gradual transference of examining to each oversea region in a growing partnership between the Syndicate and education authorities'.

SECOND WORLD WAR

After the declaration of the Second World War, the minutes of the meetings of the Syndicate began to record its impact. On 21 September, it was noted that the 1939 examination papers had already been sent in bulk to Malaya, earlier than usual; it was decided to discontinue the overseas July examinations; and there was a discussion of air raid precautions. In the next meeting (21 October) there was a discussion of a possible plan to mark overseas scripts in India and Malaya, and then send the marked scripts to South Africa. Obviously the Syndicate still envisaged this as a European war only.

The emergency arrangements for the home examinations dealt in detail with the ways invigilators had to act if an examination was interrupted by an air raid and the candidates had to go into shelters. During this period, 'every effort must be made to avoid them discussing the examination'. A report should then be written to the Syndicate to explain any special circumstances. One headmaster wrote of the effect of recent air raids on his candidates: 'Examination room behaviour showed clearly that all candidates were very tired on Tuesday 13 and Wednesday 14.' The difficulties of the individual students were noted: 'Home badly damaged . . . Home demolished (phosphorus – oil bomb) . . . Civil Defence duty all night . . . assisted in fire fighting and salvage work . . . Home demolished. Grandparents killed . . .' Those candidates whose homes were damaged, the head noted, 'have had attendant difficulties in obtaining accommodation and clothes'. The same head wrote that 'All candidates, particularly the H. S. C. candidates, showed a marked reluctance to single themselves out as undergoing special hardships when so may suffered worse, and tended to confine themselves to laconic understatements.'

The same determination that the examinations should go on as usual was to be seen overseas. In 1945 the Syndicate received a letter from the Colonial Office asking it to approve and then award certificates as appropriate to people who had taken their School Certificate Examinations while in an internment camp in Malaya. The interned Education Officer who organised 'the school' in the camp, Mr H. R. Cheeseman, wrote: 'It will mean a great deal to the candidates to get this recognition – it will mitigate the loss involved by the war and I have used the possibility of this recognition as an incentive not only to them but to the whole camp school.' Despite the difficulties of captivity, Mr Cheeseman wrote, 'the regulations of the Syndicate regarding the conduct of the examinations were strictly followed'. This episode is described more fully in chapter 4.

In another post-war report Roach mentioned the various foreign candidates who took Cambridge language examinations while they were stationed in England. Letters of appreciation had been received from Polish, Czech, Norwegian and Belgian authorities. Dutch candidates were found in South East Asia as well as in the UK where they were training with the RAF. Books were found for Dutch refugee children in England and elementary tests of their progress in English were set. There was also an initiative for prisoners of war. In April 1945, Special Lower Certificate and Preliminary tests were taken by

1,500 prisoners of war in Great Britain alone, nearly 900 of these being Italians.

REVIEW

The struggle of people to study for and take examinations in such difficult circumstances suggests how deeply the system was embedded in British culture, and also perhaps how deeply the taking of examinations resonated with something basic in a modern view of human achievement. These candidates did not have to take the exams, they wanted to take them for reasons which seemed good to them. Like the Imperial Examinations in China, the local examinations were deeply related to the culture from which they grew, a culture which valued the taking of personal responsibility and striving for self-improvement. It also valued literacy and the benefits of greater knowledge. The examinations were a way for people to express their belief in their own self-worth, based on a determination not to be judged by the place in society to which they were born. There was a strongly individual element in the taking of examinations, but society too was involved. It has been noted before that major steps in the development of the examination system in the UK were taken after wars. The School Certificate was set up after the First World War and the General Certificate of Education followed the Second. The whole system started, however, when the British performed so disastrously in the Crimean War and it was believed that a way of choosing better government administrators and military leaders had to be found.

3

HOME EXAMINATIONS AFTER 1945

HELEN AND JOHN PATRICK

POST-WAR EXAMINATION REFORM

The Second World War and its aftermath saw many proposals for reform of the education system. In particular, the Norwood Report of 1943 was the starting point for changes to the examination system in English schools which set the pattern for the next sixty years.

In October 1941, R. A. Butler, President of the Board of Education, asked Sir Cyril Norwood, Chairman of the Secondary School Examinations Council, to appoint a committee 'to consider suggested changes in the Secondary School curriculum and the question of School Examinations in relation thereto'. At the time, school examinations were controlled partly by the Board of Education, partly by teachers and partly by the university examination boards whose School Certificate and Higher School Certificate syllabuses to a large extent dictated what was taught in the senior forms of most secondary schools.

Norwood disapproved of this system. In particular, he disliked the School Certificate, normally taken at sixteen, which required candidates to study a minimum of six subjects drawn from various groups. He told the committee that a child could not receive the education which was its due 'unless there were a teaching profession free of controls and inhibitions which hampered the work'. Improvement was impossible 'if secondary school teachers were tied to an external examination'. He therefore proposed to replace School Certificate with an internal examination controlled by teachers.

W. Nalder Williams, Secretary to the Cambridge Examinations Syndicate, and a member of Norwood's committee, opposed these

200   EXAMINATION PAPERS (JUNIOR)

II.

(At 80 words per minute, 240 words to be read in 3 minutes.)

Opening a large extension of Portsmouth Grammar School,
Minutes the Home Secretary spoke of educational ideals. "What industry
¼ wants in our | schools is the development of moral character,
the imparting to a boy of the power of judgment, and, speaking
½ as | a Cabinet Minister, I would add a training in the power of
¾ concise expression. These are my three ideals in | education.
There is rather a liability in the modern forms of State education
1 to become too much in a rut. ‖ We want adventure in education.
We do not want cast iron education. There are no two men
¼ alike, and there | is no woman even like herself for more than
five minutes at a time.
½   At this school in the days | past you have educated men for
the Church and the professions. To-day industry demands that
¾ you should educate the | men to go forth as the leaders of
industry. For that you must have above all moral character. It
2 is ‖ no good placing a man at the head of a great business whose
¼ moral character may be splendid if he | cannot tell a fool from
a knave, or an honest man from either. To-day that is essential
½ in the | world. Often I have to make appointments to all kinds
¾ of offices. I do not know that my appointments are | the best,
but I strive to distinguish between the knave and the fool when
3 I have to appoint a judge." ‖

Hygiene

(Two hours)

Only six questions may be attempted.

1. Discuss the part played by water in carrying disease.

2. Explain briefly what you understand by the following:
(i) a disinfectant, (ii) accessory food factors (vitamins), (iii) a
fractured limb.

3. By what hygienic principles should you be guided in
choosing clothing suited to the climate in which you live? Why
is it necessary to change the clothes frequently?

23 School Certificate Question Paper for July 1928, Hygiene and Object
Drawing (Bound Volume 1928)

ideas. He claimed that the examination 'has improved, is improving and can be improved still further'. He agreed that it could be
abused. He particularly castigated 'the bad competitive tradition of
judging a school's progress by examination results'. He went on to
point out that, though the boards were often blamed for deficiencies
in the examination, they were only administering a system drawn

JULY 1928 201

4. What is the composition of fresh air? How is the composition of the air in a living room affected by the occupants?

5. In what ways is a severely cut leg likely to be dangerous? What precautions could you take to avoid those dangers? ·

6. Explain how flies act as carriers of disease. In what ways can we all help to prevent this spread of disease by flies?

7. What is the difference between hard and soft waters? Explain how the differences in composition of such waters are related to the sources of supply.

Object Drawing

(One hour)

The candidates should be instructed (1) *that the subject consists of the drawing board and the objects upon it*, (2) *that the subject is to be drawn in outline and may be lightly shaded in pencil*, (3) **that the drawing should fairly fill the paper provided**, *and that no credit will be given for very small drawings.*

If any of the articles mentioned cannot easily be procured, the Supervisor must use his discretion in substituting others. Full particulars of any changes made must be given on the envelope containing the drawings of the candidates.

Care must be taken that the positions of the objects are not known to the candidates beforehand.

The candidates should be placed not less than six and not more than ten feet from the objects (which should be placed 18 inches from the ground), and must sit in such a position that every one can have a fair view of the bottle.

First Group.

Objects: A half-imperial drawing board, a square prism about 15 inches in length, a bottle, and a glass tumbler.

The objects are to be placed as shewn in the sketch[1].

[1] The sketches are not reproduced in this book.

23 *(cont.)*

up by the Board of Education which 'has not seen its way to adopt constructive proposals for the improvement of the examination'. He would, he said, welcome 'a more elastic scheme of examination under which a reasonable freedom of experiment can be allowed both to examining bodies and to schools'. But he was against abolition.

24 Walter Nalder Williams, Secretary from 1921 to 1945
(Cambridge Assessment)

Nalder Williams' arguments did not prevail and in June 1943 the committee's report recommended that, after seven years' preparatory work, internal examinations should replace School Certificate. In the meantime, examining bodies should set subject-based examinations, with 'pupils taking whatever subjects they wish'. In addition, the report proposed that teachers should be responsible for writing reports on their pupils' achievements in education, 'using the term in its widest sense', to give an idea of 'the share which the pupil had taken in the general life of the school, games and societies and the like'. The committee also recommended changes to Higher School Certificate which had been criticised for trying to combine two functions – namely, selecting candidates for university scholarships, and qualifying students for university and entry to the professions. Norwood suggested that the two functions should be carried out by separate examinations, with a competitive scholarship examination and an 18 plus qualifying examination in which students should take the subjects required for their particular needs – the purpose of the 18 plus examination 'should not be to provide evidence of a "general" or "all-round" education'.

Norwood's proposals were widely criticised. The opposition was led by the Syndicate and the Oxford Delegacy. A committee of the Cambridge Syndics noted soberly that their 'general view of the relevant proposals of the Norwood committee is that they do not offer a satisfactory basis for re-shaping the school examination system'. The outspoken Joseph Brereton, soon to be Secretary of the Syndicate, urged that external examinations were 'an essential part of the machinery of education' and claimed that their replacement by internal examinations was a step which would 'allow arbitrariness, favouritism and patronage to raise their ugly heads again, and cause a much greater disintegration of the secondary system than is yet fully realised'.

Norwood argued that the boards were 'doing their best to undermine and belittle the Report from pure motives of self-interest', but he found it more difficult to counter criticism from teachers. Frank Smith, Professor of Education at Leeds, spoke of teachers' 'unwillingness . . . to shoulder the responsibility which would fall on them' if external examinations were abolished. Smith's view was supported by a poll conducted by the Oxford Delegacy which showed that 87 per cent of a total of 200 headteachers consulted opposed the abolition of external examinations at sixteen.

The teachers' response must have disappointed Norwood. He had worked to increase their role in examining and so to enhance their status as a profession, only to find many unwilling to follow his lead. But, buoyed up by the support of the Board of Education, he pressed on. In November 1943 he summoned the Secondary School Examinations Council to a two-day meeting so that he could explain his findings. When, after only two hours, he found that several members wanted to question some of the conclusions, he closed the meeting, and the Council did not meet for nearly three years. In the interim the Board of Education became a ministry and, as a result of the 1945 general election, Ellen Wilkinson replaced Butler.

Wilkinson and many of her officials were Norwood enthusiasts. In June 1946, perhaps to ease the implementation of the Norwood report, and also to punish the examination boards for their opposition to its proposals, Wilkinson removed their representatives from the Secondary School Examinations Council. She still relied 'on the co-operation of the approved examining bodies to carry out the work of the examinations', but the Council was to decide the form of the examinations without any formal input from the boards. It was their job to administer, not to initiate – a significant down-grading.

In August 1947 the new Council issued its first report. Norwood was no longer Chairman and, though it nodded in the direction of internal assessment, it went on to decree the replacement of the existing examinations for the academically able by a General Certificate of Education (GCE) at two levels – ordinary to be taken at sixteen and advanced at eighteen. Pupils could take any combination of subjects, and would get credit for every subject passed. The only grades would be pass or fail, and an O level pass was to be the equivalent of a credit in the School Certificate. There would be scholarship papers to select candidates to benefit from state or local authority funding for their university studies.

In line with Norwood's idea of reducing the influence of external examinations, the government intended O level to serve as a school leaving examination which could be bypassed by students intending to take A level, while secondary modern schools were to be free to develop their curricula without the constraints of external examinations. These policies were unsuccessful, because external examinations served too many useful functions for their demise to gain widespread support, but the idea lived on in various guises and is still debated today. Other ideas proposed by Norwood, for example, records of achievement, were also to re-emerge at later periods.

Norwood's proposals had provoked the discussion of fundamental issues which recurred in the post-war history of examinations in England. What are examinations for? How best can their purposes be met? What are their effects, intended and unintended? Who ought to control them?

INTRODUCING GCE

As part of the drive for reconstruction in the years following the Second World War, the education system was developed and reorganised. Despite the huge pressure on resources, provision was made for secondary school places for all children over the age of eleven, and in 1947 the school leaving age was raised to fifteen. The possibility of staying on at school to take external examinations at age sixteen and beyond was opened up to a great many more pupils than had been the case before the war, even though the majority could not yet take advantage of the opportunity.

The new GCE examinations were scheduled to begin in 1950, but the Minister soon realised that this did not allow enough time to make the necessary changes and postponed their introduction until 1951. James Petch, Secretary of the Joint Matriculation Board, noted sadly that 'The new Council, and the Ministry also, has found difficulty in appreciating that schools require notice of major changes in examination syllabuses and regulations and that curricula cannot be altered immediately upon the issue of a *fiat*.'

The Syndicate prepared for the new examinations. It set up a special committee on which schools taking Cambridge examinations were 'strongly represented' to report on the changes required, but it found itself 'handicapped' by the lack of direct machinery for consultation with the Secondary School Examinations Council. A feature of the new system was greater central control and co-ordination, but the examining bodies' representatives had been removed from the Council. 'As the Syndicate foretold', it noted in its 1949 report, 'this has proved to be a most serious defect in organisation', when it came to drawing up the regulations for the new examination. The examining bodies set about trying to remedy the situation, and in 1951 the Syndics were able to report the appointment of an advisory committee, on which the boards were represented by their Secretaries, which reported regularly and directly to the Secondary School Examinations Council. At the same time a change was made in the Syndicate's examination administration. In 1944 a School Examinations Committee, with school and local education authority (LEA) representatives, had been set up for an experimental period to oversee the Syndicate's UK examinations. This had proved so successful that it was incorporated into the permanent structure of the Syndicate, with a majority of teacher and LEA representatives on the Committee itself and on its subject committees.

Two features of the new examinations made the Syndicate uneasy. The first was the minimum age limit of sixteen imposed by the Minister in 1950 on the advice of the Secondary School Examinations Council. Many grammar schools had 'express' streams which took School Certificate at fifteen. These would now have either to bypass O level, or to be held back a year. Neither alternative appealed to schools. Cambridge imposed the age limit 'reluctantly', and noted a 7 per cent decrease in School Certificate entries in 1950. The age limit did not last. In 1952 the Secondary School Examinations Council gave headteachers discretion to enter younger pupils if they thought it educationally desirable. In 1953 the Syndicate had 1,922 such candidates – 7.8 per cent of the entry. Their results in academic subjects were better than those of the other candidates.

The other problem was caused by raising the O level pass to the standard of a credit in the School Certificate. Many lower-ability grammar school pupils who might have scraped passes in School Certificate were unable to achieve any significant success in O level and had little or nothing to show for their efforts. The Syndicate circulated a paper to its schools, suggesting various options designed to recognise a lower level of achievement than an O level pass. Out of seventy schools which sent in comments, fifty-eight strongly supported the Syndicate's point of view. Reaction in the press and from the teachers' associations was also favourable. The Syndics circulated the subsequent report with the teachers' comments to the Council of the Senate, and to all its participating schools, but the problem remained. In view of the anxiety in schools, the awarding committee took special care in setting the standard. The board made a special request to

schools for information about the composition of their entry, and collaborated with other GCE boards in studies to co-ordinate standards
across boards. Despite the anxiety, the proportion of passes at Ordinary level in 1953 was higher than it had been for School Certificate
credit because, the Syndicate believed, candidates could concentrate
their efforts on fewer subjects and drop their weakest ones.

It might have been expected that examination entries would fall
with the advent of GCE because of the age limit, the raising of the
pass standard to credit level and the official expectation that candidates who intended to take Advanced level would bypass Ordinary
level. On the contrary, the Syndicate found that GCE attracted more
candidates. The age limit was soon relaxed, most Advanced level candidates did take Ordinary level first, and students who might have
balked at the requirements of School Certificate or Higher School
Certificate felt able to attempt one or two subjects in the new examination. Although the Syndicate had more candidates, there were fewer
subject entries per candidate, down from an average of just over seven
in the last year of School Certificate to five in the July 1953 Ordinary
level examinations. At Advanced level there were around a third more
candidates in 1951 than had taken Higher School Certificate the year
before. After five years, as the system settled down, around two-thirds
of the Syndicate's Ordinary level candidates took six or more subjects
and less than half took seven or more. At Advanced level, around
60 per cent of candidates took three or more subjects. A legacy of
the old system was that it was still the norm for schools to take all
their examinations with a single board, so these figures probably give
a reasonably accurate view of entries per candidate.

As with any new system, the Syndicate had to revise its administrative procedures. Although the new examinations were officially
certificated as pass/fail, the Syndicate used nine numerical grades for
communicating results to schools, with grades 1 to 5 representing a
pass. The new system replaced the standardised percentage marks
used previously. It was thought to be more self-explanatory, it saved
labour and reduced the risk of errors in calculation. Arrangements
for awarding Advanced level subjects continued much as for Higher
School Certificate, but at Ordinary level the Syndicate introduced
a system of checking and re-marking samples of scripts on the pass

borderline in each subject. For a fortnight in August, senior examiners came to Cambridge to undertake this work at the premises of
the Perse School (later to become part of Syndicate Buildings at 1
Hills Road). Calculations were still needed for scholarship awards
and in 1951 the Syndicate had the use of the University Mathematical Laboratory's 'National' calculating machine. A common system
of classification of scholarship results was agreed with other boards,
and with local education authorities responsible for financial awards
to selected students. In 1953 distinctions were reintroduced at the
request of the Secondary School Examinations Council to reward
good performance and provide additional information for selection
purposes. The new examinations had brought changes in assessment
methods and there was a considerable growth in the number of examiners' visits to schools to interview candidates about their practical
work in subjects such as Geography, to assess work in subjects such
as Needlework, and to conduct tests in Cookery and administer orals
in modern languages.

THE EXPANSION AND DEVELOPMENT OF GCE

The increase in educational opportunities after the war, combined
with the greater flexibility of the examination system, provided a plat-
form for the growth of external examining. Although Cambridge was a
relatively small board in UK terms, with only around 10 per cent of the
GCE candidature after the war, home examinations constituted about
a third of the Syndicate's work. Annual Reports regularly commented
on increased demand for examinations, rising volumes of work, ever
larger numbers of examiners and papers, and, particularly from the
mid 1960s onwards, the growing rate of change in the system.

The most obvious evidence of expansion was in the number of
examination entries. In 1947, 107,356 candidates took School Certificate and 26,322 took Higher School Certificate. In 1951, there
were around 134,000 candidates at Ordinary level and around 37,000
at Advanced level. Entries grew steadily and were stimulated by the
raising of the school leaving age to sixteen in 1972. By the late 1980s,
only around 10 per cent of school leavers had no qualifications at
all. Although the available data do not allow exact comparisons over

25 Former warehouse, Combine House, Harvest Way, Cambridge, 2004
(photograph by Cameo Photography)

time, the enormous growth of external examining is not in doubt.
Apart from a plateau in the mid 1960s and a dip in the mid 1980s
following falls in the birth rate, numbers of candidates and entries
rose every year.

The Syndicate followed the general trend. In 1950, Cambridge had
nearly 16,000 candidates for School Certificate and Higher School
Certificate. A year later, for GCE, Cambridge had nearly 17,000 candidates. By the late 1980s, the figure was of the order of 200,000. The
growing number of candidates more than made up for the steady fall
in the number of subject entries per candidate.

As well as having more candidates, the Syndicate worked with an
increasing number of schools and colleges attracted by the opportunity to enter candidates for smaller numbers of subjects than
had previously been required to gain a qualification. At the end of
the Second World War, the Syndicate had 372 UK or 'home' centres entering the summer examinations for School Certificate and
Higher School Certificate. In the first year of GCE, there were

419 centres. From then on the number of home centres rose steadily. When the Durham Examination Board closed in 1964, many of its centres moved to Cambridge, which collaborated with the Oxford Delegacy in offering certificates in Oral English and in Arithmetic previously offered by Durham. By 1980 the Syndicate was dealing with well over 1,000 centres and, by the late 1980s, it was over 2,700, more than half the secondary schools in the UK. It became increasingly common for schools and colleges to enter candidates for more than one board, perhaps because they preferred a particular style of syllabus, or because a subject was not available from the board they normally used. Boards thus were able to attract entries from centres beyond their traditional clientele.

Traditionally Cambridge drew the great majority of its candidates from academically selective grammar and independent schools. In the first year of GCE over 90 per cent of the Syndicate's candidates came from these schools. But the picture soon began to change. By 1960, only 75 per cent of Syndicate candidates came from such schools. As the demand for GCE grew, the Syndicate attracted entries from technical and secondary modern schools and from further education colleges, whose needs differed from those of more academically selective schools. Although these needs were to be addressed specifically by the Associated Examining Board which was established in the 1950s, the Syndicate and other GCE awarding bodies were anxious to cater for such centres. The Syndicate also examined increasing numbers of private candidates, including those with special assessment needs, for example by providing papers in Braille.

By the end of the 1960s, the picture was different again as a result of changes in the organisation of schools in England. As the process of selection at 11 plus came to be seen as unreliable and unfair, there was a move to introduce non-selective, or comprehensive, schools. Comprehensive reorganisation usually meant that single-sex schools were replaced by mixed schools, and in some localities it was accompanied by the growth of sixth-form colleges. By the late 1980s, over 60 per cent of Syndicate entries came from comprehensive schools, and over 6 per cent from sixth-form colleges. Although the nature of the entry had changed, Cambridge still drew a higher than average percentage of its entries from selective schools – around 15 per cent, at a time when just over 9 per cent of secondary age pupils attended grammar and independent schools.

The Syndicate had long been noted for catering for girls, particularly from independent schools. When GCE started, girls comprised around half of Syndicate candidates, and they made around half the subject entries at Ordinary level and just under 40 per cent at Advanced level, compared with national entry figures of around 46 per cent and 31 per cent respectively. By 1976, around half the Syndicate entries at both Ordinary and Advanced level came from female candidates, while nationally around half the entries at O level and around 42 per cent at A level came from girls.

Another form of expansion was in the range of syllabuses and subjects developed to meet the needs of schools and candidates. When GCE was introduced there was little immediate change in the range of subjects, although there were developments in technical subjects to cater for the increasing number of candidates from technical schools and colleges. Archaeology, the History and Philosophy of Science and the History of Art were introduced in the 1950s, and Economic History in 1963. Mainstream academic subjects such as English, French, History, Geography, Mathematics, Physics, Chemistry and Biology had the largest entries at both Ordinary and Advanced level, and most candidates took straight arts or science combinations of subjects. There were strong gender differences, with arts and languages being more popular with girls, while Mathematics and sciences, with the exception of Biology, were more popular with boys. Domestic subjects were an exclusively female zone, and technical subjects a male one. These entry patterns gradually changed, with mixed arts and science combinations becoming increasingly popular and gender differences becoming less clear-cut.

In 1961 the Secondary School Examinations Council recommended that special papers should be introduced at Advanced level for the purposes of selection for university. Although the Syndicate doubted the wisdom of the plans for special papers, it recognised that Advanced level syllabuses had been criticised variously as 'too specialised', 'too pedestrian' and 'out of touch with present day knowledge', and welcomed the opportunity to re-assess what should be taught in the sixth form. Under the auspices of the Secondary

School Examinations Council and its successor the Schools Council, the examining boards worked together on a major programme of development, in collaboration with schools and colleges, subject associations such as the Joint Association of Classical Teachers and the Association for Science Education, special projects such as Mathematics in Education and Industry, and other educational bodies such as the Nuffield Foundation and the Wolfson Foundation. A system was established whereby one board could administer a new syllabus on behalf of all the boards, and syllabuses were introduced progressively as each was ready. There were developments at Ordinary level too. The Syndicate's experimental syllabuses in Advanced level Physics and Ordinary level Chemistry were taken for the first time in 1965.

In addition, the Syndicate had an ongoing programme of development and revision for existing syllabuses, often involving new approaches to assessment. Examples included increased attention to aural and oral performance in languages, with tape recordings for moderation purposes, the introduction of the option of an individual project in History, collaboration with other boards on an objective test in Economics, experiments with open book examinations and teacher assessment, and an increasing interest in assessing practical work. As alternative syllabuses became accepted as mainstream, more traditional versions were phased out. There were experiments with innovative systems of examining, including graded objectives, records of achievement and modular syllabuses (see below). Syllabuses became more informative and the style of examination papers began to change. New formats were introduced, with clearer layouts and larger, simpler fonts. There were more tables, diagrams, pictures and photographs and, by the 1980s, there was a small number of papers where candidates wrote their answers on the question paper.

There was also a range of new subjects. Advanced level Statistics, General Studies and Business Studies were examined for the first time in the 1960s. The 1970s saw the introduction of Politics, Economics and Sociology. In the 1980s, the Syndicate began offering A levels in Accounting, Computer Science, Craft Design and Technology, Public Affairs, Technical Graphics and Electronics. At Ordinary level, too, new subjects such as Home Economics, Classics in Translation and Environmental Science were introduced in the 1960s;

Electronics, Computer Studies, Economics and Integrated Science in the 1970s; and Sociology, Business Studies, Classical Civilisation, a range of combined science syllabuses, Craft Design and Technology, and Technical Graphics in the 1980s. In 1967 eleven candidates took O level Chinese at the John Mason High School in Abingdon, believed to be the first time the language had been examined as part of the curriculum of an English school.

The Syndicate prided itself on its links with its schools and colleges and these were strengthened further in the revision and development of syllabuses. Teachers on subject committees kept the Syndicate and its examiners in touch with school opinion; teachers' associations collated comments from schools about each summer's examinations; and the Syndicate regularly organised consultation exercises, conferences for teachers, exhibitions of work in art, craft and technical subjects, and visits by teacher representatives to the summer awards. The volume of such work increased in the 1980s in the run-up to the introduction of GCSE (see below). In the 1970s the Syndicate began a long association with the BBC, assessing students in further education colleges taking BBC language courses. The Syndicate relied on schools to assist in piloting new approaches to assessment and in pre-testing items for multiple-choice tests in a range of subjects. The Syndicate collaborated on the provision of materials for teachers, particularly for new school subjects, but also for old ones, for example discussing with the Joint Association of Classical Teachers how Greek texts could be kept in print. Cambridge University's Board of Extra-Mural Studies ran courses for teachers of Business Studies, with support from the Leverhulme Trust and the Institute of Directors. Courses to familiarise A level Physics teachers with the electronics required for revised syllabuses in the 1980s were held in the teaching laboratories of the Cambridge University Physics department. The Syndicate moderated the Certificate in Design and Technology Education run by British School Technology to provide updating for teachers and supported schoolteacher fellowships at Cambridge colleges.

GCE boards were answerable not only to schools but also to universities and employers. From time to time the Syndicate used their Annual Report to Cambridge University to defend their examinations

and to advertise their virtues. In debates about the sixth form curriculum and university selection stimulated in 1961 by the Secondary
School Examinations Council's proposals for special papers, the Syndicate pointed out that the 'Use of English' test which had been
introduced in 1951 to assist in the selection of candidates for scholarships had 'proved worthy to give its name to the test which is to
replace Latin as the compulsory subject for entrance to the University'. In 1963, the Syndicate was promoting the Ordinary level General paper, a forerunner of General Studies which dated from well
before the GCE, which was also used for selection for scholarships
as well as to broaden the sixth form curriculum. In the 1980s, in
conjunction with the Oxford and Cambridge Schools Examination
Board, the Syndicate began providing the Sixth Term Examination
Papers which replaced the Cambridge University colleges' entrance
examination.

In addition to offering a greater variety of examinations to a wider
range of centres and candidates, GCE boards had to ensure comparable standards across the country and to address changes in examination policy and administration. Much of this work was achieved
through co-operation between the boards in England and Wales. The
arrival of the Associated Examining Board in 1953 made a total of
nine boards, but the number returned to eight with the demise of
the Durham Board in 1964. The board Secretaries met regularly, and
took turns to host an annual conference for board staff.

The Secretaries of the GCE boards in the 1950s surely cannot have
imagined how far the boards would eventually go in agreeing common standards, policies and procedures, as well as working together on
the development of syllabuses and methods of assessment. As centres
increasingly entered candidates for examinations with more than one
board, the pressure grew to adopt common approaches. The boards
agreed on the new special papers and the official national grading
system for A level which was introduced in 1963. The use of five
pass grades, from A to E, has continued ever since. In the 1980s the
GCE boards collaborated with the Certificate of Secondary Education (CSE) boards to set up common, national centre numbers for
schools and colleges and the central database was held at Cambridge.
In the same period the boards contributed to a joint venture with the

government Department for Education and Science, subject associations and other interested parties to develop A level common subject cores, so that universities and other users would know that all those with an A level in a particular subject had studied common ground as well as material specific to their syllabus.

Cambridge worked particularly closely with the Oxford Delegacy, the Oxford and Cambridge Schools Examination Board and the Southern Universities Joint Board, sharing research and computer facilities and developing syllabuses. In the late 1970s, the Syndicate and the Southern Board merged their activities, although retaining separate identities, and, together with the Oxford Delegacy and the Oxford and Cambridge Board, they formed the Cambridge, Oxford and Southern School Examinations Council (COSSEC), signifying their intention to act jointly on a range of issues.

The boards also worked with the Schools Council and its successor, the Secondary Examinations Council. At first the Schools Council had no machinery for collaborating with the boards, but when its constitution was revised in 1966 board representatives were admitted to its committees. The Syndicate was kept busy consulting on and responding to a steady stream of proposals and initiatives from the Council. Each year the Syndicate supplied syllabuses, question papers, mark schemes and marked scripts for the Council to review. At the Council's request, boards agreed a common timetable for a number of the most popular subjects where examination clashes were causing difficulties for schools. As new subjects were introduced and more schools took examinations from more than one board, collaboration on a common timetable became increasingly necessary. In 1975, following much delay on the part of the Schools Council, an official national system of O level grades was introduced, A to E, with grades A to C being a pass. In the same year, the first autumn A levels were offered, a development facilitated for the Syndicate by the international examinations schedule at the same time of year. Prompted by concerns expressed by the boards and others that grade C at A level was too narrow and that there was not enough difference between the bottom of grade B and the top of grade D, a Secondary Examinations Council working party proposed a new method of setting grade boundaries which was introduced in 1987.

And it was not only the Schools Council whose ideas needed addressing. In 1976, for example, Prime Minister James Callaghan made a speech at Ruskin College in Oxford which sparked what became known as the 'great debate' on education. As a contribution to the debate, the Syndicate published a pamphlet on 'School Examinations and their Function', addressing current issues and setting out a list of basic questions about the purposes and nature of public examinations in the education system.

Not surprisingly, all this activity meant there was a great deal of work for the Syndicate's growing staff. There never seemed to be enough space in the Syndicate's various offices, and local schools and halls were regularly borrowed during the summer examination period to house art and craft work as well as senior examiners checking the marking of samples of scripts. New technology was used to improve reliability, accuracy, the availability of information, and the speed of processing candidates' work and results. For example, in summer 1959 samples of scripts were 'photographed or otherwise duplicated' to enable examiners to standardise their marking on identical work. In 1964 the Syndicate acquired a computer which was used in processing the summer A level examinations. Subsequently, the Syndicate's mainframe computing capacity was increased at regular intervals. The early 1970s saw trials of scoring multiple-choice tests by machine and the mid 1980s the first desktop computers. Around the same time it became possible for home centres to send in their candidate entry data on floppy disks using software written by the Syndicate for the purpose.

Some operational challenges were beyond the Syndicate's control – for example, the effects of the national rail strike in 1955. Unlike the Queen's birthday parade, there was no question of the examinations being cancelled, and emergency measures were prepared. Fortunately, the strike ended after the first few days of the examinations. Greater difficulties resulted from the postal strike of 1964, when special arrangements had to be made for distributing and collecting scripts and mark sheets across the country and, although the Advanced level results were published on the due date, the Ordinary level results were delayed.

26 Pre-computerised examination processing in the 1950s (M/P 3/2; photograph by *Cambridge Daily News*)

In 1982 the Syndicate's constitution was revised to reflect the growing divergence between home and overseas examinations. Although UK standards underpinned international standards, home and overseas examinations increasingly served different constituencies. The Council for Home Examinations was set up in 1982, as a committee of the Syndicate, with a membership which represented UK interests, including Syndics, members of boards of examining bodies with which the Syndicate had close connections, teachers and local education authority officers.

NEW EXAMINATIONS FOR THE SIXTH FORM

Higher School Certificate subjects could be taken at two levels, principal and subsidiary, with subsidiary comprising half a principal subject. Candidates commonly sat a mix of the two levels, a practice which added breadth to their studies. The Advanced GCE had no subsidiary level, and O*, or Alternative Ordinary, was introduced instead. The most popular subjects offered by the Syndicate at this level were the general paper, Human Biology and English, but overall entries for the examination were disappointing. At best, it only offered the candidate an additional O level pass, even though it was a specifically sixth form qualification. Concern was expressed that in many schools the sixth form curriculum was now too narrow and, in 1969, the Schools Council proposed a new two-step examination with papers at 'Qualifying' and 'Further' levels. This scheme met so much opposition that it was soon abandoned. They replaced it with a structure of five subjects which would be examined after one year at 'Normal' level with two to be tested after two years at 'Further' level. The Syndicate was unenthusiastic. In response to the Schools Council questionnaire circulated in 1974, the Syndics voiced 'serious qualifications about the opportunities provided for those sixth-form pupils who are able and wish to specialise'. They argued that 'a combination of four subjects taken at A (or main) and AO or subsidiary levels . . . would lead to a greater degree of flexibility and a simpler structure'. This was the preferred option of the majority of teachers they had consulted. Discussions dragged on. In 1978 the Syndics noted that 'the total set of N and F material to date covers 2,324 pages which compares – at least in length – with the 1,224 double-column pages of the Revised Edition of the Holy Bible'. Finally, after all this effort, in 1980 the Department of Education and Science announced that they would not approve the scheme.

In 1984 the government made another attempt to broaden the sixth form curriculum. They announced the introduction of Advanced Supplementary examinations. The syllabuses would be the same standard as A level, but cover only half the content. They would be studied over two years and two of them would count as the equivalent of one A level. The universities agreed to treat an AS as half an A level for admissions purposes. The Syndicate offered a full range of syllabuses, both on its own account and in conjunction with the other boards in the Cambridge, Oxford and Southern School Examinations Council. The first examinations were sat in 1989, by which time there was a suite of seventeen AS syllabuses across the curriculum.

Proponents of the new examination had hoped that a significant proportion of A level candidates would offer a mix of complementary and contrasting A level and AS subjects, but in 1989 the Syndicate reported that the examination had not lived up to expectation. In 1989 AS attracted only 5,226 candidate entries, compared with about 43,000 A level entries. The overwhelming majority of candidates for university entrance continued to offer three subjects at Advanced level. Candidates found that preparing two half-syllabuses was significantly more demanding than preparing one whole one. So the take-up of the new examination remained disappointing until it was swallowed up in the reforms instituted in Curriculum 2000.

In the early 1970s there was a move from the boards offering the Certificate of Secondary Education to extend certification beyond age sixteen. In 1974 the Schools Council circulated a proposal to interested bodies for a new 17 plus examination – the Certificate of Extended Education (CEE). It was intended for candidates whose 16 plus qualifications were no better than CSE Grade 2. The Syndicate's response was unequivocal. They were 'in favour of . . . a Certificate of Extended Education and wish to be involved in examining at this level'. The examination was to consist of five papers examining a one-year syllabus, and the three Oxford and Cambridge boards, later joined by London and the Southern Universities Joint Board, agreed to co-operate to produce ten subject syllabuses to be examined for the first time in 1977 'if the new examination is approved'. It was not approved, but the boards were allowed to run a pilot examination in 1977. It was agreed that a Certificate of Extended Education grade 3 would be the equivalent of a CSE grade 1 and a C in GCE. The number of entries for the new examination was 'predictably' low, given that it was not certain to be approved – 326 candidates and 341 subject entries – but the boards persisted with it and the entries grew. The government was far from committed to the Certificate of Extended Education and appointed the Keohane Committee to consider its future. In 1980 the committee reported in favour of its continuation, and foresaw an entry of 50,000 by 1991. The government was unimpressed and in 1981 announced that the Certificate of Extended Education would only continue until the new structure of examining at 16 plus was in place. It believed that the needs of Certificate of Extended Education candidates could be better served by vocational examinations, perhaps in the form of the Certificate of Pre-Vocational Education. In fact the five boards continued to offer the Certificate of Extended Education until 1990, by which time the entry was around 5,000.

CERTIFICATE OF SECONDARY EDUCATION

GCE O level was designed for the top 20 per cent of the ability range, and initially the majority of candidates came from selective grammar schools. But students attending secondary modern schools also wanted formal, external recognition for their achievements. Increasing numbers took O levels and a range of other qualifications offered by national bodies such as the Royal Society of Arts (RSA) and City and Guilds, and by local organisations. The Ministry of Education wanted to minimise the impact of external examinations on the curriculum and resisted pressure from parents, students and employers to approve examinations on a national scale which would meet the needs of secondary modern school students. The pressure reached a head following a series of official reports on aspects of secondary education, culminating in the Beloe Report in 1960. There was general support for Beloe's proposals and the Minister of Education accepted the principle of a new examination.

The Certificate of Secondary Education was a subject-based examination for sixteen-year-olds, to be awarded at the end of a two-year course. It was aimed at the 40 per cent of the ability range below the 20 per cent for whom O level was deemed suitable. There were three modes – mode 1, where the examination board designed the syllabuses and set the assessment; mode 2, where the school designed the syllabus and the board set the assessment; and mode 3, where the school designed both the syllabus and the assessment, with board validation. CSE was organised by fourteen regional examination boards in England and Wales, with local teachers taking the lead in curriculum and syllabus development. There was a rush to be ready for the first examinations in 1965. The East Midlands Regional Examinations Board (EMREB), for example, did not receive official recognition until August 1963, so the first candidates had less than two years to prepare. The popularity of the new examination was not in doubt. CSE subject entries more than quadrupled in five years, rising from 230,977 in 1965 to 982,721 in 1969. Following the raising of the school leaving age in 1972 there was a further rise and by 1977 there were 2,782,300 subject entries.

GCE boards such as the Syndicate were not directly involved in CSE, but both GCE and CSE came under the aegis of the same government-appointed regulator, the Schools Council. They were also linked in terms of standards – a grade 1 at CSE was deemed equivalent to an O level pass, and the East Midland Board, for example, collected statistics on candidates who took the same subjects at both CSE and GCE to monitor equivalence. In 1964 the government Department of Education and Science expressed concern that the pattern of entry for GCE might be affected by the introduction of CSE and wrote to the GCE boards stating that they should take this into account in determining the O level pass/fail point. In 1966 and 1968 the Syndicate surveyed schools, asking them how many subject entries they had made for CSE which previously would have been made for O level. Although the percentage of Syndicate entries which had been affected rose between 1966 and 1968, it was still small, at 4.3 per cent, and in well over half of the centres surveyed the introduction of CSE had not affected O level entries in any way.

TOWARDS THE SIXTEEN PLUS

As grammar and secondary modern schools were increasingly replaced by comprehensive schools from the late 1960s, the existence of two systems of examinations in the same schools seemed anomalous. It was not always easy to select the more appropriate course for students, and it was difficult to establish parity of esteem between grade 1 at CSE and a pass at O level. In 1970 the Schools Council proposed a single examination system at 16 plus and set up a working party to investigate the implications. The Syndicate believed that the wide range of ability would pose serious problems, but in 1971 they began to co-operate with the East Anglian CSE Board in experimental work. A year later the South Western CSE Board joined them. In 1973 the East Anglian Board and Cambridge produced experimental common papers in five subjects and in 1974 the South Western Board and Cambridge joint papers appeared, together with joint papers in craft subjects produced by Cambridge and the East Midland Board.

These experimental papers, taken by a handful of schools, did not remove the Syndics' doubts about the feasibility of common examinations. They wrote in their 1975 report: 'It is practicable for the two Boards to work together in preparing tests for a wide ability range. The examinations appear to have met the needs of the average candidates, but the Syndicate have expressed doubts as to whether a common examination is suitable both for the less able students and for those proceeding to Advanced level.'

Meanwhile, a Schools Council sub-committee produced a report arguing that a common examination was feasible. Cambridge was still not convinced: 'Such examinations . . . will not extend the able children. In addition they have proved difficult and unsuitable for students of below average ability.' The Syndics favoured 'a common *system* of examination which would permit different tests to be used for students with different skills and abilities. The existing GCE and CSE examinations, if based on joint syllabuses and a common grading scheme, would go far towards meeting the needs of schools.'

The GCE and CSE boards had good reasons to tread carefully when considering a common examination at 16 plus. Who would administer such an examination? GCE boards could draw candidates from any part of the country, while CSE boards were limited to tight geographical areas. Would the new examination be regional, in which case the CSE boards might be called on to administer it, or country-wide, when the task might fall to the GCE bodies? Cambridge made its view clear. It noted that, at a conference called to discuss the Schools Council report, support was expressed for freedom of choice of examining board and for maintaining the university connection in the administration of 16 plus examinations. There was resistance to the regionalisation of existing GCE boards. Another problem was the popularity of CSE mode 3 examinations which were teacher set and assessed. In 1977 nearly a quarter of CSE examinations were mode 3 and the Syndicate doubted if such internal examinations could serve the same functions as the largely external examinations which constituted the GCE.

Whatever its reservations, Cambridge, in partnership with the East Anglian Board, continued to develop common papers. The feasibility studies were ended, and new joint examinations were offered to all schools in 1977 as an alternative to GCE and CSE papers. Shirley Williams, the Education Secretary, watched such developments with some unease. She argued that the public had confidence in GCE and CSE, and felt that this confidence was too valuable to put at risk. So she appointed a committee under Sir James Waddell to consider examining at 16 plus and issue recommendations. Sir James reported in 1978. He endorsed the plans for a single 16 plus examination, based on integrating existing GCE and CSE grades. Three or four regional consortia of combined GCE and CSE boards should administer the examination, and national criteria should be drawn up to define subject titles and coverage. He favoured differentiated papers to cope with the wide ability range. He thought that the new courses should be on offer by 1983, with the first examinations in 1985. The government accepted his recommendations.

The Syndics cannot have been pleased by Waddell's recommendations. They were particularly dubious about the new examining groups. 'How it will be possible for a GCE board both to amalgamate with other boards for one purpose and to maintain a separate existence for others has yet to be explained', they noted, sourly. Though Cambridge had often co-operated with other boards, and the Syndicate and the Southern Universities Joint Board had agreed to merge their activities, the Syndicate had kept its own identity. But whatever their feelings, events pressed them forward. In 1979 it was agreed that the Midland region should provide one of the groups for the new examination and in 1980 representatives of the Cambridge, Oxford and Southern School Examinations Council met those of the local CSE boards. Colin White, chairperson of the East Midland Board Examinations Committee, remembered that they 'tip-toed gently round each other, like the first missionaries meeting the first cannibals'. In 1981 the Midland Examining Group (MEG) was set up, consisting of the Syndicate, the Oxford and Cambridge Board, the Southern Board, the East Midland Board and the West Midlands Board. Although the new groups had a regional basis, schools were not tied to their 'home' region but could enter pupils for any group's examinations. Soon group officers were at work setting joint CSE/GCE papers with a new urgency and there were discussions in the Cambridge, Oxford and Southern School Examinations Council and the Midland Examining Group on the implications of examining in a multi-cultural society and catering for candidates with special assessment needs. Group officers were also co-operating with representatives of other groups to draw up the national criteria governing the new examination.

Meanwhile the government was sending out conflicting signals. In 1980 the answer to a planted question in the House of Commons gave the impression that the common examination was on its way, but in 1982 Sir Keith Joseph, the Education Secretary, made it clear that he had not come to a final decision. Examining bodies remembered the fate of the N and F proposals and wondered if history was about to repeat itself. Then, quite unexpectedly, in June 1984, Sir Keith announced that he was in favour of GCSE, and fixed 1988 as the first year of the new examination. Time was short. Teaching for the new examination had to begin in 1986, and it was not until 1985 that the National Criteria were approved by the Minister. Once schools realised that GCSE was inevitable, they turned increasingly to the joint GCE/CSE papers set by the new groups. In their 1986 report, the Syndics noted that 4,000 centres were taking Midland Examining Group examinations. Of these, 2,900 were outside the Midland region, and of these 2,000 were Syndicate centres. The Syndics saw the increasing number of candidates for the joint examinations as helping to pave the way for GCSE.

By the end of June 1986 more than seventy Midland Group GCSE syllabuses had been approved and the Syndicate was involved in an intensive programme of teacher training for the new examination. One-day courses on course work were most in demand. For the first time a minimum of 20 per cent of the assessment was to be based on course work and many teachers had no experience in this field. 'Teachers want to know the nature of course work . . . and in particular the exact details of how they should go about assessing it', so the Midland Group's nationwide programme of courses was 'warmly welcomed'.

The Midland Group was competing for candidates with the other examining groups and, until the entries were in, nobody could be quite sure how well they were doing. It was therefore with some relief that the Syndics were able to report in April 1988 that the Midland Group had attracted 1.6 million subject entries, 'much higher than expected'. This number of candidates put a heavy strain on the Syndicate's resources. For home examinations at all levels, the Syndics reported, some 1.8 million separate papers/components were handled by the Syndicate, landing on the desks of about a third of a million candidates in over 2,600 Syndicate centres throughout the United Kingdom. It proved impossible to retain this market share as each syllabus revision encouraged schools and colleges to look at what the different groups offered and perhaps change provider. The number of Midland Group subject entries fell to 1.3 million in 1997 and to 1.1 million in 1998 because of 'intense competition' following yet another round of examining body re-organisation, which included the merger of the Midland Group with Oxford, Cambridge and RSA Examinations (OCR, see below). In 1999 the Syndics reported that the OCR share of GCSE candidates stood at 23 per cent but 'GCSE generates a satisfactory financial return'.

27 A Level Performing Art students at Joseph Chamberlain College, 1989
(UCLES Annual Report, 1990)

THE IMPACT OF GCSE

The GCSE examination had several novel features. First, it was much
more tightly controlled than O level, with national and subject criteria and regulations. As GCSE developed, the degree of regulation
increased and some of the approaches, such as 100 per cent coursework
schemes, which were permitted in 1988 were subsequently outlawed.
The GCSE groups worked closely together to co-ordinate their activities, setting up the Joint Council for the GCSE. Following a revision
of the syllabuses for the 1992 examinations, however, scrutinies of
grade awarding by the regulator and by Her Majesty's Inspectorate
found inconsistencies of approach and recommended greater uniformity. A code of practice covering administrative and awarding procedures was introduced in 1993 and became statutory in 1994. This
was part of a general move to assert central control over the education
system. The Schools Council, which had been allowed to use its initiative, was abolished in 1984 and replaced by a succession of bodies

under closer government control, and in 1988 a government-approved national curriculum was introduced.

Second, GCSE was available across the whole ability range. This was unprecedented. Even the joint GCE/CSE papers had been designed for the top 60 per cent or so. It was to prove difficult to design papers suitable for all and a range of approaches was tried, including different forms of tiered papers designed for different parts of the ability range. Here, too, experimentation was eventually replaced by a more uniform system where most syllabuses had two tiers.

Next, it had been hoped that the new examination could be criterion referenced: that is, designed to identify, more precisely than traditional examinations did, what candidates knew, understood and could do. The idea was investigated in various ways but, as with other attempts to apply the concept of criterion referencing in general educational assessment, it proved unwieldy and impractical, and had to be dropped. Elements persisted, however, in the form of grade descriptions.

Finally, GCSE had to serve as the assessment vehicle for Key Stage 4 of the national curriculum. This involved further extensive revision of syllabuses for summer 1994, and the linking of the seven GCSE grades, A to G, to the ten levels of the national curriculum. Syllabuses changed again when the curriculum was revised in 1998, and there were further revisions for 2003. Such revisions had to fit into a government-imposed timetable which, the Syndics complained, was 'extremely tight'. Entries in subjects such as Design and Technology rose and fell according to whether they were a compulsory part of the national curriculum. GCSE results were important for career choice and also figured largely in school performance tables. As a result, there was a rapid growth in enquiries and appeals. Gradually the Syndicate came to terms with GCSE and with developments such as short courses equivalent to half a GCSE, vocational GCSEs, and entry level certificates for students working below the level of GCSE. When Oxford, Cambridge and RSA Examinations was set up, changes to the board's structure and to its computing and administrative systems made 1998 a particularly challenging summer, but the following year the Syndicate referred to the administration of GCSE as 'relatively trouble-free'.

A LEVEL BEFORE AND AFTER CURRICULUM 2000

While the examining bodies were facing the challenge of GCSE, they continued to promote developments in A level and to plan for the effect of GCSE and the national curriculum on A level syllabuses in the longer term. The GCE boards worked together on identifying good practice in GCE examinations, but their work was overtaken in 1992 by a regulatory document setting out A/AS principles. The GCSE code of practice was soon followed by a GCE code. The two codes were later merged and extended to include vocational qualifications.

There had long been concern in the UK about vocational education and qualifications, and various government initiatives had attempted to improve provision in this area. In 1995 the government commissioned Sir Ron Dearing to consider the framework for qualifications for the sixteen-to-nineteen age group. His report, *A Review of Qualifications for 16–19 Year Olds*, was published in 1996. The key recommendations were that: A level and AS should be restructured; AS should be replaced by an Advanced Subsidiary level; there should be a new Advanced Vocational Certificate of Education and vocational GCSEs in parallel to the general qualifications; and there should be closer integration between academic and vocational qualifications and the bodies which awarded them.

In many ways, the Syndicate was well placed to meet the challenges posed by the Dearing review and the government proposals which followed it. The new A and AS levels were to be modular in structure, with examinations held twice a year. There would be three modules for AS and a further three, known as A2, to make up a full A level. The AS was to be set at the standard expected of students part way through an A level course. The Syndicate had long had an interest in modular assessment. Building on developments arising out of the government-funded Technical, Vocational and Educational Initiative in the 1980s, the Syndicate had set up the A level Modular Bank System, with the first examinations taken in 1989. Despite uncertainty as to whether the government regulator would allow modular schemes in the long term, entries rose, and a new suite of syllabuses, known as Cambridge Modular A Levels, was introduced in the 1990s. The Midland Examining

28 The Craft Hall at 1 Hills Road during Art marking, 1980s (M/P 5/8;
photograph by Peter Askem)

Group offered modular GCSEs, and the Syndicate's experience of modular assessment structures was further enhanced by the mergers with the Oxford Delegacy and the Oxford and Cambridge Board which also had successful schemes.

A second feature of the new system was the government's desire to reduce the number of awarding bodies so as to improve comparability and enable tighter central control. Cambridge had already made a major contribution to this aim. The Southern Universities Joint Board had merged with the Syndicate in 1990 and its separate operations were closed down. In 1994 the University of Oxford agreed to sell its interest in the Southern GCSE group to the Associated Examining Board, and its A level interests, in the shape of the Oxford Delegacy and the Oxford and Cambridge Schools Examination Board, were merged with the Syndicate. The three suites of A levels, with their different cultures, which the Cambridge group now ran from two offices in Oxford and two in Cambridge, were marketed under the banner of Oxford and Cambridge Examinations and Assessment

Council (OCEAC). Although steps were taken to monitor comparability of standards and procedures across the suites, rationalisation on a major basis awaited the outcome of the Dearing review. The mergers, however, paved the way for the unitary awarding bodies which were to follow.

Where Cambridge was less well placed was in the field of general vocational qualifications. The government wanted to raise the profile and esteem of vocationally oriented qualifications and, as well as reducing the number of awarding bodies, it proposed that they should be unitary, that is, responsible for the full range of school and college general qualifications – GCSE, GCE and General National Vocational Qualifications (GNVQ). Each unitary awarding body would have to include at least one academic and one vocational body. The Syndicate had only limited experience in the field of vocational qualifications: at the request of the University, it had awarded a Certificate of Proficiency in Laboratory Technique in conjunction with the Cambridgeshire Technical College and School of Art for a brief period in the 1940s and 1950s; it had developed syllabuses in subjects which catered specifically for technical school and college students and for members of the armed forces; through the Midland Examining Group, it had participated in the Technical and Vocational Educational Initiative. But now it needed a more vocationally oriented partner. The Syndicate had a long-standing relationship with the Royal Society of Arts (RSA) in the field of English as a foreign language, and the Midland Group had co-operated with the RSA in the provision of a small number of GCSE syllabuses. Following the Dearing review, the Syndicate had established a partnership with the RSA Examinations Board, and the UK work of the two organisations was merged with the formation of Oxford Cambridge and RSA Examinations at the end of 1997.

Although the Dearing review was published in 1996, there was much consultation, discussion and change of policy before what came to be known as Curriculum 2000 was implemented, with the first AS examinations being taken in 2001. It was hoped that the new Advanced Subsidiary qualification would broaden the sixth form curriculum. Students were to be encouraged to take four or five subsidiary subjects in the first year of the sixth form before specialising

29 Progress House, Coventry, 2004 (photograph by Cameo Photography)

in the second year. But there were implications for timetabling and resources in schools and colleges, concerns that examination courses would push non-examination activities out of the curriculum and fears of over-assessment with three years of examinations in a row, at ages sixteen, seventeen and eighteen.

There were also concerns about standards. If the AS was to be at a standard lower than A level, would the A2 part of the full A level have to be harder? If all examinations were modular, what was to stop candidates repeatedly re-sitting modules? How could candidates get an overview of a subject if they could tackle the course and the assessment one module at a time? Critics argued that existing modular syllabuses were less demanding than the more traditional 'linear' A levels because the pass rates were better. Awarding bodies suggested that the pass rates were better because candidates who were failing did not finish the course. Complex rules and regulations were drawn up to address such concerns, and it was difficult for awarding bodies to finalise the new syllabuses while the rules were still under debate. At the same time, awarding bodies were getting to grips with the development of the new vocational qualifications, which had their own rules, and advanced extension awards which were to replace special papers.

The biggest problem was that there was no time to pilot the new structure. The awarding bodies had to mark, grade and issue the results for the first AS examinations with little evidence as to what the standard of the AS should be and how it would relate to the final A level results the following year. Like other changes in the examination system, the introduction of Curriculum 2000 prompted schools and colleges to evaluate the new syllabuses and perhaps change awarding bodies, adding to existing uncertainties about what kinds of candidates the new examination was likely to attract. The awarding bodies tried to ensure that candidates were not penalised in any way by being the first cohort to take a new examination, but at the same time they were duty-bound to maintain standards from previous years. For the first time, evidence of prior achievement, in this case GCSE results, was used as a measure of the calibre of the candidates entering the new examinations, a development made possible by the boards' arranging central data collection which was organised by the Syndicate. Even so, difficulties in awarding the first new A levels in the summer of 2002 were the subject of an enquiry led by Mike Tomlinson, formerly Chief Inspector of Schools. The challenge of establishing the standard of a new qualification was thoroughly aired in his report and in the accompanying press reports.

CONCLUSION

Bill Brown, Deputy Secretary of the West Midlands Examinations Board, wrote in 1990: 'Examining is at its most comfortable when it becomes repetitive, tried and tested, familiar and predictable. It rests easily within an education system in which the imperative to conservatism is strong.'

Since the Second World War, examining bodies have had to live in an environment full of new initiatives and unexpected twists and turns. The Syndicate has come through all the ups and downs. In the 1950s it was a relatively small player in the UK. Now, OCR is one of the three unitary awarding bodies in England, building on the strengths of the past and adapting to the needs of the future.

Sir Cyril Norwood cannot have imagined how spectacularly he was swimming against the tide in his efforts to curtail examinations and their impact. Today there are more examinations in more subjects taken by more candidates than ever before.

4

INTERNATIONAL EXAMINATIONS
AFTER 1945

GREG LACEY

On 18 October 1945, Walter Nalder Williams, Secretary of the Syndicate, received a letter from the Colonial Office enclosing details of unofficial School Certificate Examinations that had been conducted by detainees in the Sime Road internment camp in Singapore during January and August of that year. One of the detainees was H. R. Cheeseman, Deputy Director of Education in Malaya at the time of the Japanese invasion in 1941–2. Almost as soon as the war ended, he sent a report to the Colonial Office to ask for its help in approaching the Syndicate with the request for official recognition of the examinations, that he, as acting local secretary, had organised. Subsequently he also forwarded the question papers and marked scripts. The story told in his report was truly remarkable. It described how courses for adult internees had at first been organised, but that these were forbidden by the Japanese from October 1943, when they became nervous about a class being offered in Radio Theory. Thereafter, at first in secret, but from July 1944 with Japanese permission, schooling continued for children only. Instructors in most subjects, with the relevant teaching experience, could be found from amongst the inmates, but conditions were harsh. Textbooks and other equipment were in very short supply, lessons had to take place outside in what little shade could be found on the site, and time for teaching could only be found after the normal day's 'fatigues' (generally four hours' gardening labour) had been completed. Not surprisingly, Cheeseman concluded that: 'the conditions in the camp were most unsatisfactory for boys. They heard and saw much that should not have been seen or heard by them . . . The inevitable repression acted unfavourably on young life . . . The chief disability was undoubtedly the low mental condition of instructors and candidates, owing mainly to diet and environment, though there were also the other unavoidable handicaps of captivity.'

However, despite the fact that 'no copy of the Regulations for the School Certificate Examination [were] available', it was possible to prepare a small number of candidates for examinations of School Certificate level that were set and marked by the instructors. Cheeseman warned the candidates that there could be no guarantee that the Syndicate would officially recognise their efforts, but promised that an application would be made on their behalf.

Following receipt of the Colonial Office letter, that application was considered by the Oversea Committee of the Syndicate on 2 November, which, having taken advice from its examiners who had scrutinised the scripts, gratifyingly concluded that School Certificates should be issued. Similar awards were also made to internees in camps in Shanghai.

The story of the Sime Road detention camp examinations illustrates well the importance of Syndicate examinations and the esteem in which they were held, notwithstanding the suspension of the overseas School Certificate for the duration of the war. However, although the Syndicate moved rapidly at the end of 1945 to resume its international examinations, not all of the consequences of the Second World War for the Syndicate would be as straightforward to resolve. The political impacts of the war, and most notably the impetus it gave to the decolonisation movement, would usher in a period of continuous and fundamental change, both in the nature of the examinations offered by the Syndicate, and in the customers to whom they would offer them.

POST-WAR DEVELOPMENTS

As the de facto examination board to the colonies, the Syndicate had long-established working relationships both with education authorities in the individual colonies themselves, and with the Colonial Office. During the inter-war period the principle that examinations would need to be modified to match local needs had been accepted, and significant syllabus changes had occurred, particularly with the

SIME ROAD SCHOOL CERTIFICATE EXAMINATION.

ARRANGEMENTS: The arrangements for the Examination, following the scheme suggested to the Syndicate after the outbreak of the war in Europe (for use if question papers were lost), were carried out under the direction of Mr H.R.Cheeseman,Deputy Director of Education, Malaya, who acted as Examinations Secretary.

DISABILITIES: The special disabilities of the candidates were :-
(1) lack of privacy for study (due to communal dwelling and greatly restricted accommodation - lessons had to be taken in the open air and so constant distractions and frequent cancellations of lessons owing to weather were inevitable, while seating and tables had to be improvised: these and general Camp conditions militated against satisfactory preparation of work by instructors and pupils) (2) lack of text-books and books of reference: the few text-books available were shared - the subject that suffered most from lack of material was History, (3) scarcity of writing paper: written work had to be reduced to the minimum and it will be appreciated that this was a very serious handicap, (4) enforced changes in the personnel of instructors: the teaching undertaken was additional to the ordinary Camp physical fatigues and, owing to the strain involved teachers were constantly resigning (the subjects most affected by this were Mathematics (four changes) and History (three changes)), and the incidence of sickness and indisposition among the instructors and the candidates involved (at a low estimate) the loss of 25% of the time available for teaching. But the chief disability was undoubtedly the low mental condition of instructors and candidates, owing mainly to diet and environment, though there were also the other unavoidable handicaps of captivity.

SYLLABUS etc: There was no copy of the Regulations for the School Certificate Examination available but a Syllabus was drawn up and the requirements of the examination (including details of the question papers) compiled with the assistance of teachers of long and also recent experience with School Certificate classes. It was decided to set and mark papers strictly in accordance with what were regarded as the normal requirements of the Syndicate. The scheme of marking was as follows:- B. (Bad failure) 25% and less, F. (failure) 26% up to but not including 33⅓%, W. (Weak Pass) 33⅓% to 40% inclusive, P. (Pass) 41% to 50% both inclusive, C.(Pass with Credit) 51% to 60% both inclusive, G. (Good) 61% to 74% both inclusive, A. (Very Good) 75% upwards.

EXAMINATION CENTRES: Centre 1. (Girls) Presiding Examiner, Miss C.E. Renton (Johore Education Service); Centre 2 , (Boys) Presiding Examiner- Mr H.R.Cheeseman. The regulations of the Syndicate regarding the conduct of the examinations were strictly followed. The question papers were typed under conditions of secrecy and each set of question papers was placed in a sealed envelope which was opened in the presence of the candidates five minutes before the time fixed for the beginning of the paper. Candidates were authorized to write on both sides of the paper and it was necessary to use writing paper varying in size and quality. The examinations were held from 15th to 27th January 1945,excluding Sunday 21st January.

PANEL OF EXAMINERS AND DETAILS OF QUESTION PAPERS: The details of the time allotted to each paper, the number and choice of questions, and the rubrics for each paper are shown in the set of question papers attached. It is hoped that these will be found to correspond with the recent requirements of the Syndicate. Mr H.R.Cheeseman acted as Moderator for the Examination as a whole and for the English section. The schedules attached include the confidential mark sheet and a statement of the results as notified to the candidates. When the candidates were informed of their results, they were told that application would be made for the examination to be accepted by the Malayan Governments and by the University of Cambridge Local Examinations but that no assurance provision of a much wider range of languages examinations. The School Certificate Regulations for 1946 give a good idea of the ways in which local circumstances could be accommodated:

Special papers are regularly set for individual schools or areas in Economics, Navigation, Agricultural Science and Rural Science. History papers on a special syllabus are set for the Trinidad Education department (West Indian History), for Achimota College, Gold Coast, and for Gordon Memorial College, Khartoum. Special Arithmetic papers are set in December only with questions based on (a) Indian currency, (b) Mauritius currency, (c) Sudan currency and weights and measures, (d) metric weights and measures (for Argentina).

Post-war, as independence for the colonies approached, the whole issue of localisation of the examinations became an urgent matter. But what exactly would localisation mean? As countries achieved independence, they naturally wanted to assume control of school examinations, and the Syndicate was both sympathetic to this aim, and willing to offer help in bringing it about.

But control could mean many different things, and certainly was not something that could be achieved overnight. In July 1961, just before his retirement, Joseph Brereton, Syndicate Secretary since 1945, and therefore the man who had led the organisation during the early years of the localisation process, set down a blueprint for his successors on the stages in the creation of what he termed 'Oversea Examination Councils'. He identified five main phases in the 'transfer of responsibility . . . to a local examining body':

- an 'original stage', during which UK examinations would be administered by the Examinations Section of the local Ministry of Education.
- a 'centralising stage', during which a central organisation is established to conduct UK examinations, and in which some local marking of papers set specially for the area might take place.
- Examinations Council (first stage), during which an independent organisation is established, generally with the participation of local universities and colleges, with further development of local syllabuses and marking, and special regulations applying to the specific country or area.

- Examinations Council (second stage), during which the Council takes over the administration and marking of the local school leaving examination, but final control over standards and syllabuses still rests with Cambridge.
- Examinations Council (final stage), in which the involvement of Cambridge ends, and the Council administrates a completely independent examinations system.

By the time Brereton was writing this document, several countries were well advanced in this process. The West African Examinations Council had been established in 1952 to conduct school examinations in Ghana, Nigeria, the Gambia and Sierra Leone, and by 1961 was responsible for the marking of around a third of the scripts, and for setting about a quarter of the question papers in the West African School Certificate Examination. The Sudan Examinations Council had been set up in 1954, and was running the Sudan School Certificate Examination for 2,000 candidates a year (though from Cambridge's perspective this was one of the less successful of the localisation projects as the Council was disbanded in 1962 when the government assumed direct control over the conduct of school examinations). In Malaya, shortly after independence in 1957, the Federal government had set up a Federal Examinations Syndicate, which, amongst a wide range of responsibilities for other school examinations, worked with the Syndicate in the provision of the School Certificate Examination. In the years following Brereton's retirement, other areas such as East Africa also took the path of localisation, but he can hardly have imagined that this facet of the Syndicate's work would last until the end of the century and into the next, with major programmes completed or still ongoing in Zimbabwe, Botswana, Namibia, Swaziland, Singapore, Brunei and elsewhere.

A WIDER RANGE OF INTERNATIONAL EXAMINATIONS

It must be obvious that, over the sixty or more years since the Second World War, there have been many changes in the examinations that the Syndicate has offered internationally, yet there has also been a

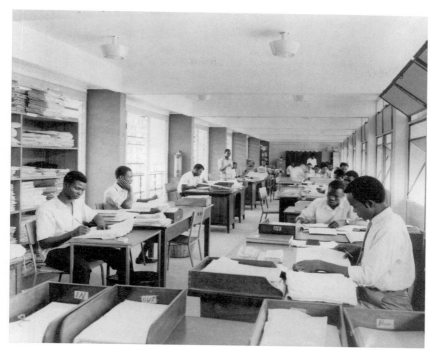

31 Offices of the West African Examinations Council, Lagos, 1964 (M/P 1/7)

surprising strand of continuity. In the immediate post-war years, the most significant examination for school leavers was still the School Certificate (SC). This was a 'group' examination in which candidates had to reach a satisfactory standard in at least six subjects, including English Language, to be awarded the certificate. There was also a 'Junior', that is lower-level, certificate, but this was examined for the last time in 1953. The Higher School Certificate (HSC) was also offered, but taken initially by relatively small numbers of candidates. In 1951, for example, there were over 18,000 candidates for the School Certificate, but fewer than 1,000 for the Higher School Certificate. With localisation, variations in the School Certificate requirements for specific areas emerged, such as the inclusion of compulsory Malay Language for candidates from the Federation of Malaya.

32 Home Economics examination at St Mary's School, Kuching, Sarawak,
1956 (M/P 1/6)

However, there were factors other than localisation which led
to changes in the Syndicate's international examinations, not least
changes in the UK itself, such as the introduction of GCE (replacing
School Certificate / Higher School Certificate) in the UK from 1951.
GCE was a subject-based examination, with none of the School Certificate / Higher School Certificate group requirements. The Syndicate Annual Report for 1952 acknowledged that what would in future
be the 'Oversea School Certificate' would have to be modified, and
set down three basic purposes of such changes:

- to adapt the examinations so that they better reflected the needs of
  different areas;
- to keep in line with UK examinations in order to maintain
  comparability;
- to encourage private schools overseas to broaden their curricula.

33 Craftwork examination at the Teachers' Training College at Nasinu, Fiji, 1956 (M/P 1/6)

What is most notable, of course, is that the School Certificate / Higher School Certificate was not abandoned overseas. The international status and credibility of these qualifications would have made their immediate replacement by GCE impossible, but there was in any case no will to do this. However, over time, the Syndicate moved to integrate some features of the GCE examinations into the School Certificate / Higher School Certificate structure. The first change came in 1955 with the replacement of standardised marks by the nine-point GCE grading scale. More importantly, by 1959 the Oversea School Certificate was being offered in many areas as a joint School Certificate / O level examination, the main significance of which was that School Certificate candidates could (given certain restrictions) be awarded a certificate showing their results in individual subjects, even if they failed to satisfy the group requirements of the School

Certificate. In the years that followed, the differences between GCE and School Certificate / Higher School Certificate became in practice less and less significant, but some countries using Syndicate examinations, such as Mauritius, have retained their preference for a group examination, and their candidates are still awarded School / Higher School Certificates. Surendra Bissoondoyal, former Director of the Mauritius Examinations Syndicate, writing in 1998, explained that, while localisation was entirely feasible, given the more flexible approach of the Syndicate to local requirements and the conservative nature of Mauritian society which places a high value on internationally recognised and portable qualifications, a clear-headed decision had been taken not to disrupt arrangements which were operating satisfactorily.

Meanwhile in 1988, a further round of examination reform in the UK had replaced the O level examination with the General Certificate of Secondary Education (GCSE) (see chapter 3). Amongst other aims, GCSE was intended to provide a single examination for candidates of all abilities to replace the dual O Level / Certificate of Secondary Education system, and to include within the new syllabuses many of the educational ideas and approaches, such as assessed coursework, that had been developing since the introduction of GCE. These aims were equally valid within the international context. For other clients, the Syndicate developed the International General Certificate of Secondary Education (IGCSE), which has recently celebrated its twentieth anniversary. The new examination adopted the educational philosophy of the GCSE reforms, but adapted to the needs of international schools. At the time, the Syndicate was the only UK examining board to offer this, and thereby achieved a much wider presence amongst English-medium schools of an international type than had hitherto been the case. At a time when its traditional business, conducted through Ministries of Education, was declining rapidly because of localisation, the success of IGCSE was a welcome and significant development. By the end of the twentieth century, the demand for English-medium education was developing rapidly, and the availability of a standard, internationally recognised qualification at 16 plus was appreciated by such schools, not least for providing them with a coherent curriculum structure for students of that age group. Recognising that individual schools, scattered around the world, would need

34 Celebrations for the 20th anniversary of IGCSE, Cambridge 2005
(Cambridge International Examinations; photograph by Nigel Luckhurst)

ready access to help and advice about this new examination, the Syndicate set up the IGCSE Office, which for around fifteen years acted as a point of contact for IGCSE centres, as well as arranging conferences and training events. Thus, although GCE examinations both at O and A level continued to be provided post-1988, the O level examination was, apart from in those countries that wished to retain it, rapidly superseded by IGCSE.

At that time no similar change occurred at A level. Without the stimulus of UK curriculum reform it proved much harder for the Syndicate successfully to innovate at 18 plus, and in international schools it also faced well-established opposition from the International Baccalaureate. During the 1990s an attempt was made to launch the Advanced International Certificate of Education (AICE) as a higher-level qualification developing from IGCSE, but it failed to achieve the popularity of its lower-level equivalent. The Higher IGCSE (HIGCSE) was also developed in the 1990s, specifically as a university entrance level qualification for centres in Southern Africa, but localisation in the countries concerned effectively removed the demand for it. Thus, by the early twenty-first century, the A level examination was still the Syndicate's main international qualification at 18 plus, although considerably modified to keep its comparability with UK examinations, most notably in the introduction of the dual AS/A2 (see chapter 3) structure from 2000 onwards.

The existence of IGCSE also provided an alternative to O level as a model for a new crop of countries that, during the 1990s, were moving towards localisation. Its suitability for all candidates was a particularly attractive feature, offering alternative examination papers for candidates of different levels of ability. Namibia became the first country to use the IGCSE curriculum, as a transitional stage in developing its own localised examination based on IGCSE principles. Swaziland, having long used School Certificate / O level, is currently switching to IGCSE as a basis for its own localisation, with a target date of 2011 for completion. Other countries, such as Botswana, have already completed this process. Elsewhere, IGCSE has been used by countries as a means to modernise UK-style curricula offered in specific groups of schools. For example, in Egypt, where the Ministry of Education had previously permitted a small number of English-medium private schools to offer O level examinations, IGCSE is now offered in schools of this type under the terms of a tripartite agreement between the Syndicate, the Ministry of Education and the British Council. The original agreement, signed in 1990, allowed for six schools to teach the IGCSE curriculum, but placed upon the Syndicate the responsibility for inspecting these schools to check their suitability and effectiveness as IGCSE teaching centres. The British Council in Egypt is responsible for organising the conduct of the examinations themselves. The tripartite agreement has been regularly updated since 1990, and the number of schools in the scheme is now over sixty.

However, although much of IGCSE's success has been in replacing O level with a more modern alternative, it is interesting to note some of the points of continuity it offers with its predecessors. Indeed, the Syndicate's educational aims in introducing IGCSE can be seen as directly comparable to those stated in 1952 for the ongoing modification of the School Certificate examination. For example, an important feature of IGCSE was the preservation of the idea of a group examination, albeit on an optional, additional basis. IGCSE is a single-subject examination, but in order to encourage candidates to study a broad, balanced curriculum, an additional group qualification, the International Certificate of Education (ICE), was awarded to candidates satisfying the requirement to pass in at least seven subjects, including Maths, two languages, a science, a creative subject and a Humanities subject.

DIVERSIFICATION

Originally international examinations were just Cambridge UK examinations offered internationally. In the words of A. A. Adeyinka: 'Between 1910 and 1925, . . . the Cambridge Syndicate operated its examination programmes in Nigeria without review, modification or adaptation to local needs'. However, the pressures of localisation and the widely differing requirements of different customers meant that in the post-war era the Syndicate had to develop means of responding to, and consulting with, those who used its examinations. In 1945 it established the Advisory Committee for Oversea Examinations, which for many years remained the guiding influence behind international developments. One of its first actions was to issue a statement to all areas outlining plans to establish local consultative procedures, 'emphasising the importance attached by the Syndicate to the appointment in every area of a local organisation on which the school teachers are strongly represented'. In practice it took some considerable time for these plans to be carried out, as not until 1955 were the four Area Advisory Committees (for India/Pakistan, the Caribbean, Malaya and East/Central Africa) set up, and even then meetings were at first held in the UK. The first overseas meetings were in 1961, in East Africa, and then later in the year in the Caribbean. In addition to this formal structure for consultation, from 1955 the Syndicate also organised an annual conference in Cambridge on overseas examinations. Over the years these conferences were attended by representatives from most of the areas in which Syndicate examinations were offered – for the most part, the representatives were teachers being

35 Caribbean Secondary Schools Conference, 1955 (M/P 1/5)

trained in the UK at the time – and they gave the Syndicate valuable opportunities to gain opinions first-hand on significant issues, such as the modification of School Certificate Examinations to bring them more in line with GCE (considered at the 1957 conference).

The idea of annual conferences was revived in the late 1980s with the advent of IGCSE. The novelty of this examination made it essential for the Syndicate to organise training events for teachers, to explain syllabus requirements and, more specifically, to train them as course-work assessors. To these ends, a residential conference took place at Robinson College, Cambridge, each July throughout the 1990s, attended on average by 100 or so IGCSE teachers from schools around the world. Although most of the work at these conferences was conducted in subject groups, they also provided invaluable opportunities for Syndicate examiners and staff to meet IGCSE teachers and hear their views on the examinations. As with the earlier annual conferences, a limitation was that they were attended only by people who could be in the UK at the relevant time, which meant that they were not necessarily representative of IGCSE teachers as a whole, and could not effectively satisfy the training needs of teachers from all countries. Accordingly the Syndicate began to organise more and more training events outside of the UK, as well as participating actively in conferences organised by other educational bodies, such as the European Council for International Schools (ECIS).

The processes of localisation also created many new training needs. The creation of the new examining bodies presupposed that it would be feasible to recruit competent bureaucracies to run them, and the Syndicate was active in providing the necessary support. From as early as 1953, examinations officers from the West African and Sudan Examinations Councils were spending time in Cambridge, being trained in the different aspects of the administration of examinations. The character of such 'study leave' visits broadened over time, so that by the early 1960s small numbers of overseas examiners were coming to Cambridge to take part in the marking of examinations. Although such visits continued on an ad hoc basis, by the later 1980s it had become increasingly clear that demand existed for a more formalised, in-depth training programme, not necessarily tied to a specific localisation exercise, but available for examinations professionals from around the world. Accordingly, during the 1990s, the Syndicate offered residential courses, twice a year, covering all aspects of the conduct of examinations, both administrative and subject-based, theoretical and practical. In 1993, for example, courses in Cambridge were attended by personnel from countries as far apart as Bulgaria, the Gambia, Latvia, Sri Lanka and Thailand, not all of which were traditional users of Syndicate examinations. In addition to training programmes, the Syndicate also developed a software program called the Small Examinations Processing System, designed to assist small states in administering their own examinations. This has been installed in the Bahamas, Botswana, Lesotho and Swaziland.

Nonetheless, during the various phases of localisation, the numbers of overseas administrators and examiners being trained in Cambridge have always been hugely outnumbered by the numbers being trained

by Cambridge staff 'in-country'. This is particularly true of the stage
at which a country or area begins to take over the marking of its own
scripts, and subsequently the setting of its question papers and the
devising of syllabuses. The often large numbers to be trained in these
activities have always made it more cost-effective for the Syndicate
to send its own examiners to the countries in question to conduct
the necessary training workshops. Thus, by 1965, Syndicate staff and
examiners had made over 100 visits to West Africa as part of the localisation programme there. Indeed, given the subsequent localisations in
so many other countries, it is hardly an exaggeration to suggest that
almost all the Syndicate's most senior examiners during the latter
part of the twentieth century must have had at least one opportunity
to travel overseas, and many became seasoned international travellers.
It is hard to exaggerate the benefits of these visits for all participants:
the trainees, self-evidently, being equipped with the skills required to
run their own national examinations, but the trainers, too, having the
opportunity to learn from the experience of working with colleagues
from different cultures and educational experiences.

EXTERNAL INFLUENCES

It must be evident that the Syndicate's international activities since
1945 have been shaped considerably by the impact of events and developments – some predictable and long-term, such as the achievement of
independence, which brought with it localisation of examinations, but
others unpredictable, although their effects on the Syndicate could be
almost as important. The Suez Crisis of 1956, for example, by clos-
ing the Suez Canal until April 1957, demonstrated the vulnerability
of the sea communications on which the Syndicate depended for the
despatch of question papers, candidates' scripts and subsequently the
examination results. Tom Wyatt (who was to become Syndicate Secretary in 1961) was visiting India in late 1956 and found widespread
concern in the schools that the School Certificate results might be
delayed. It was therefore at this time that the Syndicate's first experiments with air mail occurred, though the rituals of packing overseas
question papers in boxes and then into mailbags for despatch on the
next steamer departing from Tilbury would continue well into the

36 UCLES examination papers arriving in Zimbabwe and being sorted for despatch to the regions under the supervision of the Zimbabwe Ministry of Education and Syndicate staff, 1993 (*UCLES Annual Review*, 1993)

latter 1960s.[1] It was the renewed closure of the Suez Canal in 1967 because of the Six-Day War that finally convinced the Syndicate to move to air mail.

Transit and storage prior to examinations is always a potentially weak point, whatever the means of transport. In 1981 there was a spectacular leak in which five genuine and two fake papers were published ahead of the examinations in the local press of one of the countries where they were taken. It transpired that they had also been available for purchase by candidates. The papers were withdrawn worldwide and replaced at a cost of more than £190,000. Then, as now, elaborate precautions existed to ensure the integrity of the whole examining process: the use of security printers to produce papers; strict

---

[1] Interview by the author with John Attwood, 9 May 2006. Mr Attwood joined UCLES from school in 1946, and, apart from his period of National Service, was employed there all his working life. For most of this time he worked in the Question Paper Despatch section.

rules governing invigilation and the handling of papers and scripts. Nevertheless this traumatic event ushered in yet more stringent security measures in Cambridge and a complete overhaul of examination administration in the country concerned.

The Falklands War of 1982 posed a direct threat to the continuation of Syndicate examinations in Argentina. Before that date a small number of schools had taken Syndicate courses, though the examinations themselves were conducted through the British Council. The war meant that the Council closed its offices, and, whilst the schools wished to maintain the link with Cambridge, it was not immediately clear how this might be achieved. Most of the schools were members of the English-speaking Scholastic Association of the River Plate (ESSARP), which approached the Syndicate for permission to take over the administration of the examinations in Argentina. However, according to Peter Stoyle, who was the Association's President at the time, even once permission was gained, significant problems remained.

In the aftermath of the war it was not possible to make bank transfers overseas, nor could documents such as examination papers be sent directly into the country from the UK . . . It was clear that the atmosphere created by the war would reduce the number of candidates, but no-one had any realistic idea of how many entries there would be . . . Once schools had paid their examination fees, large amounts of cash in dollars had to be taken to a local exchange house which was in a position to send funds to the UK. That this was something of a risky affair was shown when once, after due payment had been made, and those concerned were relaxing over a coffee in a downtown bar, thieves entered and stole the treasurer's briefcase from under his seat! The next problem was how to get the question papers into the country and send the scripts back to Cambridge for marking. This had to be done by having the papers brought to Montevideo and taken into Argentina by car from Uruguay, with similar procedures having to be adopted for the despatch of scripts.[2]

Even when relations between Britain and Argentina were restored, the Association continued to run the Cambridge school examinations, and

---

[2] Note from Peter Stoyle to the author, 15 May 2006. My thanks are also due to Mr Jimmy Cappanera, who chaired the Cambridge Examinations Committee in Argentina for many years, for providing additional detail about the conduct of UCLES examinations during the period after the Falklands War.

during the 1980s and 1990s was an active partner with the Syndicate in supervising the rapid growth of examination entries that followed the introduction of the IGCSE curriculum.

The first official visit to Zimbabwe (then Southern Rhodesia) by Syndicate representatives took place in December 1964. In the aftermath of the collapse of the Central African Federation, Sir Ivor Jennings (Chairman of the Syndicate) and Victor Hardy (Deputy Secretary) found themselves dealing with officials of the Rhodesia Front government that was to make a Unilateral Declaration of Independence (UDI) from Britain in the following year. It was already clear that the Rhodesian government was planning to align its education system with standards in the Republic of South Africa, and in particular with South African matriculation. This would be bad news for the Syndicate as the School Certificate Examination was perceived as being at too low a level for university entry, and the proposal was to adopt the GCE O level offered by the Associated Examining Board (AEB) instead. Zambia and Malawi (the other former members of the Central African Federation), which both achieved independence in 1964, had also considered making the same change, but had ultimately decided to stick with the School Certificate Examination, which offered a wider range of pass grades – an important matter given the planned expansion of education post-independence. In fact, the switch to the Associated Examining Board by the Smith government ultimately proved to be an enormous stroke of good fortune for the Syndicate. Because the Associated Examining Board examinations were associated with the white regime in Rhodesia, once Zimbabwe moved towards full independence following the Lancaster House Conference of 1979, it was a natural step for the new majority government to reintroduce Cambridge examinations as an interim measure before designing its own system of qualifications. The immediate introduction of universal secondary education in Zimbabwe meant that candidate numbers were extremely large – for example, in 1984 there were over 100,000 candidates for O level English Language, a figure that had risen to around 180,000 by 1991. Thus, at a time when many of the Syndicate's other traditional customers were already localised or were moving rapidly towards it, Zimbabwe immediately became the Syndicate's largest customer. There was some irony in the fact that, in the same year that the Zambian Examinations Council took over full control of its own localised examinations (1981), the Syndicate commenced its consultative role in advising the Zimbabwean government on the establishment of its own Zimbabwean National Certificate of Education, a process that would take nearly another twenty years to complete.

Another good example of the impact of events concerns Singapore, one of the countries with which the Syndicate has enjoyed the longest and closest co-operation. Prior to Malayan independence in 1957, both Singapore and Malaya had entered candidates for the Overseas School Certificate Examination. However, Malaya's independence sparked a series of developments which would eventually lead to the establishment of Singapore's own O level, examined for the first time in 1971. Plans for a Malayan School Certificate Examination had been made prior to independence, and the first examination took place in 1957. It was similar to the standard Overseas School Certificate, but replaced the compulsory English Language examination with Malay Language. By 1962 it had become possible to take all subjects in the Malay medium, though for the time being the English-medium alternative continued to be offered. Meanwhile, Singapore was moving rapidly towards its own independence. It achieved full internal self-government in 1959, and discussions soon began with Malaya over the creation of Malaysia, which came into being in 1963. Although Singapore retained control over its own education policy, in the longer term the expectation must have been that it would make some moves towards rationalising its education provision with the rest of Malaysia. This never happened. For a complex set of reasons, Singapore left Malaysia in 1965, and became an independent state in its own right. Agreement was soon reached with the Syndicate over a joint Singapore–Cambridge O level examination, in which question papers would all be offered not only in English, but also in Chinese, Malay and Tamil. Singapore itself would administer the examinations in the three local languages, and the Syndicate those taken in English. This co-operation was extended to GCE A level for the 1975 examination, and in 1984 to a new examination – the N (Normal) level – designed specifically by Singapore as a pre-O level qualifying examination. Subsequently, Singapore has moved to localise its examinations, but this has taken a rather different form from that

37 David Barrett, Syndicate subject officer, visiting Temasek Junior College, Singapore, 1992 (*UCLES Annual Review*, 1992)

in most other countries. The current arrangements have passed ultimate control over syllabus development, question papers and grading standards to the Singapore Ministry of Education, with the Syndicate still responsible for most aspects of the administration of the examinations, including the marking of candidates' scripts. Singapore is now the Syndicate's largest single customer. In the intervening years, Malaysia fully localised its examinations, offering all subjects in the Malay medium only from 1978 onwards, and cutting most links with the Syndicate, though around 400,000 candidates a year still take a joint Malaysia–Cambridge O level English Language examination. Interestingly, the recent decision by the Malaysian government to permit the teaching of Maths and Sciences in the English medium has brought about a renewed collaboration between the Syndicate and the Malaysian Examinations Syndicate in setting questions in

38 Bahamas examination room, 1948 (M/P 1/2)

English for its Sijil Pelajaran Malaysia (SPM), the Malaysian Certificate of Education, i.e. O level equivalent examination.

Another small state confronted by the same choice between localisation or continuance of the Cambridge link opted for a rather different
half-way house. The Bahamas Board of Education, which had introduced its own Junior Certificate Examination in 1953, began to move
towards a Bahamian examination for secondary school leavers in the
1970s. The Ministry of Education decided, however, that the Bahamas
General Certificate of Secondary Education (BGCSE) introduced in
1993 should be accredited each year by the Syndicate. Certificates
bear both the crest of the Bahamian government and that of the
Syndicate.

RECENT DEVELOPMENTS

Since the 1990s, the Syndicate has made strenuous efforts to diversify its international activities. Though its core business of school

39 Meeting between local examinations officers and John Sadler from the Syndicate's International Division in the Bahamas, 1992 (*UCLES Annual Review*, 1992)

examinations has in fact proven remarkably resilient, the impact of localisation programmes has ultimately been to bring to an end a large proportion of the work done in co-operation with Ministries of Education. The Syndicate has actively had to seek new clients, and be prepared to offer new services. Initially this meant the provision of vocational qualifications, notably in the area of Information and Communications Technology (ICT), but more recently there have been moves away from the business of assessment and into the provision of educational resources and training. Technological change has meant that the Syndicate can now provide many of these services on-line – a far cry from the not too distant past when many of its customers would have had to rely on postal communications for their contacts with Cambridge. Indeed, new technology has already begun to have an impact on traditional modes of assessment too, with the introduction of on-line marking of candidates' scripts, and moves to develop on-line testing, accessible whenever it is required.

40 Students studying science in Brunei (*UCLES Annual Review*, 1992)

CONCLUSION

To summarise the importance of the Syndicate's international work in the period covered by this chapter is no easy matter. The world has changed enormously, in almost every way imaginable, and the Syndicate has had to accommodate and embrace these changes. Its work today, particularly in the nature of the services it offers and in its relationships with its clients, is radically different from how it operated in the immediate post-Second World War years. Yet it is hard to imagine that the Syndicate could have achieved its current position without the status and esteem, still less without the network of working relationships around the world, established during its time as the semi-official examining board of the colonies. These left it almost uniquely well placed to take advantage of the rapid expansion of English-medium education that started in the latter part of the

41 Victoria International School, Tanzania, 1993 (*UCLES Annual Review*, 1994)

last century and continues today, creating a new market for English curricula and qualifications, just at the time that it sought to replace business lost through the processes of decolonisation. The broader legacy, both of the Syndicate's colonial role, and of the localisation processes that ensued, has undoubtedly been significant. Professor A.J. Stockwell has commented that:

The overseas expansion of UK examination systems was an aspect of the dissemination of English language, Western values and British power to the non-European world. Some may indeed argue that the export of British educational standards fell into the category of 'cultural imperialism' . . . . UK-controlled examinations came to determine both the content and the method of English-medium education in the colonies . . . These examinations performed an important administrative function for, without the army of clerks who were recruited locally from those holding the 'Cambridge Certificate', colonial rule would have been less secure, and the process of decolonisation more disruptive, than was generally the case.

Greg Lacey

The colonial period is now past, but much of Professor Stockwell's comment remains relevant to the present day. The values implicit in a western, liberal education, the hard currency of qualifications that are accepted internationally as rigorous and impartial, and the status of English as a world language, remain the touchstones of the Syndicate's continuing importance to its international customers.

5

ENGLISH LANGUAGE EXAMINATIONS

PETER FALVEY

INTRODUCTION

Readers will note, from previous chapters, that the English language examinations offered by the University of Cambridge Local Examinations Syndicate are referred to as English language examinations or EFL examinations. This was a traditional form of labelling until relatively recently when the concept of EFL (English as a Foreign Language) was superseded by the label ESOL (English for Speakers of Other Languages). ESOL is a more generic label than EFL as it encompasses not only those candidates for whom English is a foreign language, such as a Mandarin speaker, but also those for whom English might be a second, or other, language, like someone from the Commonwealth for whom English is a second language or someone who speaks a mother tongue and a further language but also uses English as a third (other) language. This change was reflected in the re-naming of EFL Examinations to Cambridge ESOL in 2002. The labels ESOL and EFL or Examinations in English will be used as appropriate for the period being described.

This chapter chronicles the beginning of EFL examinations at Cambridge with the introduction of the Cambridge Certificate of Proficiency in English (CPE) examination and the introduction, development and growth of further examinations in English for Speakers of Other Languages (ESOL) as English emerged as the world's second language, especially in science, commerce and travel. The chapter will describe the development of English examinations and their rapid growth in the last quarter of a century. The contrast between the original Cambridge approaches and those of the premier

American English language examination institution, Educational Testing Service Princeton (ETS), will also be discussed, as will recent developments.

The Certificate of Proficiency in English examination was a comparative newcomer in the context of all Cambridge examinations. It was not introduced until 1913, fifty-five years after the first Cambridge examinations were held. The first reference to what became the CPE emerged on 8 March 1911 in a request from the University's Council of the Senate to the Syndicate asking it to institute a Teaching Certificate in Modern Languages. This request had emerged from an earlier request from the Modern Languages Association to the University asking them to establish teaching certificates 'testing the knowledge of Modern Languages possessed by teachers, or those who intend to be teachers, of those subjects'. Many of these teachers did not possess a degree. In the minute of 30 January 1911 no mention was made of a teaching certificate in English as a Foreign Language. After the request of 8 March, almost a year's deliberation followed, involving the Secretary, James Flather, who corresponded with various individuals as well as the Modern Languages Association about syllabus outlines for Modern Languages and English certificates. There seems to be no evidence as to why English was added to the original brief. As a result of Flather's work, the General Purposes Committee of the Syndicate recommended, on 1 February 1912, that the Syndicate establish Certificates of Proficiency in French and German, English for Foreign Students and Religious Knowledge – all to be in association with the Cambridge Higher Examinations. The first English as a Foreign Language examination thus owed its origins to a request from the Council of the Senate to investigate setting up a certificate in Modern Languages which somehow became extended to include an English certificate. Thus, we can speculate that the CPE emerged from a request to develop a certificate for teachers of English, not as a test of language proficiency for other learners of English.

The CPE's murky beginnings are revealed in the papers of Jack Roach, an assiduous chronicler and supporter of EFL examinations, who reported in 1944 that no one seemed to know why the Syndicate started the examination. He even speculated that it might have been a breakaway from an English language examination offered to non-university candidates by the University of London and commented that both the London and Cambridge examinations were based on a course for foreigners, that both were heavily academic, with a paper on Phonetics, and both had the same examiner, Professor Daniel Jones.

Based on what appear to be unclear reasons, it is fascinating that the introduction of a new examination by the Syndicate, one supposedly 'based on a course for foreigners', should herald the beginnings of what would become a major, new and successful testing and assessment industry. Nowadays, testing and assessment specialists would heavily criticise the development of such an examination, on the grounds that it lacks a clear set of assessment specifications. L. F. Bachman and A. S. Palmer in *Language Testing in Practice* mention three activities in setting examinations tasks: describing the specific vocabulary and grammar likely to be required by candidates as a basis for designing language test tasks; providing a detailed description of the language that will be used in the different test tasks that are set, so that the language in the variety of tasks set is comparatively similar, thus ensuring reliability; and comparing the characteristics of the target language use and test tasks to assess the authenticity of the tasks.

However, hindsight often fails to consider the context in which decisions to introduce examinations are made. The Syndicate, no doubt, was responding, as it had done in 1858, to an external request, just as it often does nowadays, although nowadays the Syndicate is not merely responsive but often proactive in noting new developments – such as recent advances in information technology using interactive methods of assessment – so that they can anticipate and plan for new examinations before the requests arise.

In its first five decades, the growth of the CPE was inhibited by the outbreak of the 1914–18 and 1939–45 wars, but even between the wars – in the words of Roach – 'it teetered along with 14 or 15 candidates a year'. In 1923 there were 13 candidates; 15 years later there were 675, of whom 212 sat the CPE overseas. By the end of the Second World War, in 1945, the number of UK candidates was fewer than in 1928 but overseas candidature had increased to 972. By 1960, there were almost 8,000 candidates, growing steadily until 1980 when there were almost 20,000, a figure which had more than doubled by 2001 to 48,514.

We have seen that the Certificate of Proficiency in English was introduced on the eve of the First World War. Co-incidentally, a lower examination in English proficiency, the First Certificate in English (FCE) was created on the eve of the Second World War. It was originally named the Lower Certificate in English. Introduced in 1939, it evolved in various ways in the decades after the Second World War, alongside its older sibling. Major revisions occurred in 1975 (when it was renamed First Certificate), in 1984 and in 1996. In 2006 the examination underwent further review and limited modifications will also be made in 2008. The First Certificate contains five papers with a similar format to the CPE. The use of the title 'First Certificate' did not rule out the development of lower forms of an English proficiency test, as new names for lower-level examinations, such as Preliminary English Test 1980 (PET) and Key English Test 1994 (KET), were created and are now in common use.

The CPE had been running for twenty-six years before the FCE examination was introduced. This slow progress contrasts strongly with the rapid test development that Cambridge ESOL implemented in the 1980s and 1990s.

SECOND WORLD WAR

After the declaration of the Second World War, the minutes of the meetings of the Syndicate began to record its impact, as one can see in chapter 2. Roach mentioned the various foreign candidates who took Cambridge language examinations while they were stationed in England. There was also an initiative for prisoners of war. In April 1945, Special Lower Certificate and Preliminary tests were taken by 1,500 prisoners of war in Great Britain alone, nearly 900 of these being Italians. A sombre incident was reported in 1944 in the Cambridge Examinations in English section of the Annual Report: 'Reported Proficiency entries from Czechs, Poles and French in Stalag Luft III; one of the candidates was among the 47 officers shot "while escaping".'

42 Students studying for the Cambridge First Certificate in English at EF
International Schools, Hills Road, Cambridge, 2007 (photograph by
Nigel Luckhurst)

In contrast, a different event occurred just after the war when Miss
Herdman of the British Red Cross wrote to Cambridge apologising
for the absence of Indian prisoners of war who had not turned up for
the examination because they had heard, just the previous day, that
they were all going to be repatriated.

WAR ORGANISATION
of the
BRITISH RED CROSS SOCIETY and ORDER OF ST. JOHN OF JERUSALEM

PRISONERS OF WAR DEPARTMENT.
Chairman :
MAJOR-GENERAL SIR RICHARD HOWARD-VYSE, K.C.M.G., D.S.O.

Educational Books Section :
Chairman :
THE MASTER OF BALLIOL.

TELEPHONE:
OXFORD 47850

Director :
MISS E. HERDMAN, M.A.

THE NEW BODLEIAN.

OXFORD.

Assistant Director :
BRIGADIER H. F. DAWES, D.S.O., M.C.

MHFC/ME.   June 16th, 1945.
                                            EXAMINATIONS
J.O. Roach, Esq.,   Rec. 1 9 JUN 1945
Syndicate Buildings,
Cambridge.   Ans.
                     School Certificate
Dear Mr. Roach,

        Thank you for your letter L/R 4028 of
May 25th, which in the press of work has
not been acknowledged.   We wish the scheme
for Indian Prisoners of War could have been
started earlier, as we are sure that many
of them would have benefited by it, but in
the circumstances we cannot be surprised
that all the men want to get home without
delay.

        We feel that you have been put to a
great deal for nothing in the end, and would
wish to thank you very much for what you
did, and for what you were prepared to do.

            Yours sincerely,

                E. Herdman

43 Letter explaining the absence of Indian POWs from the examination from
Miss E. Herdman, British Red Cross, to J. O. Roach, June 1945 (PP/JOR 1/1a
xxvi)

Although the candidature for the Certificate of Proficiency in English grew in the last two decades of the twentieth century, it should be noted that other, newer ESOL examinations grew even more rapidly in those years. This is not because the CPE was less attractive to candidates and their teachers, but because it is a difficult examination. It sets a high standard of proficiency, one that is not appropriate for everyone's needs. Indeed, for many years the Certificate of Proficiency in English was used in countries such as Greece, and regions such as Latin America, as a benchmark for teachers of English whose mother tongue was not English. Only later did specialist examinations for teachers of English replace the Certificate of Proficiency in English. Comparatively few of the world's ESOL speakers can aspire to the proficiency levels assessed at CPE level but English is still required even by those who cannot reach those levels without large amounts of application of time and money. The development of the First Certificate in 1939 assuaged some concerns about the need for a lower test of proficiency but it was the huge growth of the travel industry and the use of English as an international language for commerce, industry and technology that created a need for English at lower, more functional levels, for those who would otherwise be deemed competent or growing in competence, but who would not be deemed fully proficient.

When describing the changes made to the Certificate of Proficiency in English over the years, we can see that the first examination of the CPE was not unlike those examinations given to native speakers of English. Indeed, paper 4 in the CPE Written Paper was originally taken from a UK-based examination for native speakers of English. At that time, the Proficiency examination consisted of five written papers and two oral examinations, the whole lasting twelve hours.

The first Certificate of Proficiency in English examination was heavily literature- and culture-bound. The literature topics for 1913 included 'The effect of political movements upon nineteenth-century literature in England and English Pre-Raphaelitism' and were very Anglo-centric. By 1930, when a special literature paper was provided for foreign students, the Anglo-centrism of 1913 had been tempered with topics such as 'The topic that is most discussed in your country at the present time' and 'Fascism'.

Proficiency

BRITISH
LIFE AND
INSTITUTIONS
16 DEC. 1964
Morning
3 *hours*

UNIVERSITY OF CAMBRIDGE

LOCAL EXAMINATIONS SYNDICATE

Certificate of Proficiency in English

BRITISH LIFE AND INSTITUTIONS

(*Three hours*)

Answer **five** *questions*

(*Not more than* **two** *questions may be chosen from Part II*)

Part I

1. What is the importance of the fact that there is official recognition of the existence of an Opposition in the British Parliamentary system? How is that recognition shown?

2. What are Juvenile Courts in Great Britain and how do they work?

3. Give a brief account of the principal functions of the Home Secretary.

4. What are the main differences between a Rate and a Tax? What arguments have been advanced for merging the two?

5. How does the Committee system operate in an English County Council?

6. What are the principal problems which are having to be faced by the emergent Commonwealth countries in Africa?

7. What is a Commonwealth Conference, who usually presides over it and what is its importance?

8. What is the "rule of law" and how does the British Constitution exemplify it?

9. Account briefly for the fact that British Railways in the post-war years have been running at a loss.

[**TURN OVER**

Nº 1788

44 Certificate of Proficiency in English paper on British Life and Institutions, December 1964 (Bound Volume 1964)

2

Part II

*(Not more than **two** questions to be answered from this Part)*

10. Enumerate the various Bank Holidays in Great Britain and say why they are sometimes important for the pattern of holidays there.

11. Give a brief account of any **one** social service offered by the State in Great Britain.

12. What is Subtopia and what problems has it created?

13. What is the "eleven plus" examination and why is there a demand for its abolition?

14. Why has Great Britain decided on the establishment of a National Theatre and why has it taken so long to do so?

15. What is the High Street of a country town and what are its typical features?

44 *(cont.)*

CHANGES TO THE CERTIFICATE
OF PROFICIENCY IN ENGLISH AFTER 1975

Although there were changes to the Certificate of Proficiency in English syllabus between 1945 and 1975, literature and translation papers were as much in evidence as language papers. It was not until the 1975 revisions that the CPE began to resemble the CPE of today. The work of N. Chomsky in Linguistics, J. R. Firth in Applied Linguistics, and D. Hymes and M. A. K. Halliday in Sociolinguistics began to focus on language and, in particular, language in use rather than the study of language as a system. With the growth in world travel and the need for practical, day-to-day interaction between English language users, there also emerged the concept of *language as communication*, with journal articles by authors such as Henry Widdowson and books on English for Specific Purposes which produced titles such as *English for Engineering* and *English for Agriculture*. These

changes were reflected in the CPE 1975 revision which featured papers
in listening comprehension, reading comprehension and speaking.
The translation and non-linguistic studies papers would, over time,
become optional papers, not a compulsory part of the examination.
The 1975 CPE examination consisted of five papers. C. Weir and M.
Milanovic provide a detailed account of the introduction, development and revisions of the CPE from 1913 to 2002 in *Continuity and
Innovation: Revising the Cambridge Proficiency in English Examination
1913–2002.*

CHANGING THEORIES AND THEIR EFFECT
ON CAMBRIDGE ESOL EXAMINATIONS

We have already seen how changes to the CPE were affected by emerging attitudes to language use, especially language as communication.
However, at the same time, external influences, outside the UK, also
had an effect on Cambridge ESOL examinations. A major influence
was the approach to testing which became prevalent in America, for
two reasons. One was the influence of testers of intelligence. The
other was the overpowering attitude towards fairness in all examinations manifested through the concept of reliability in examinations.
What this, in essence, meant was that marking should be, first of all,
objective (hence the growth of objective, multiple-choice tests), not
liable to the whims of individual examiners, and, secondly, reliable,
in that the results obtained in one test by a candidate should, on the
whole, be replicated in a further test with an allowance for further
learning, natural development and so on. This approach is called the
psychometric approach.

   In the UK the introduction and use of objective testing in English
language examinations and other Cambridge examinations was much
later than elsewhere because there already existed a long-standing,
traditional form of testing, namely the essay. An even longer tradition
of testing was, of course, used by Chinese civil servants centuries ago
in the entrance examinations for the Chinese civil service. Candidates
wishing to become mandarins, senior civil servants, were accommodated in huts, specially prepared for the exercise, and told to write
down all they knew, emerging only after they had finished telling of

all they knew. In the UK, the essay form, together with oral examinations, which followed the European tradition of *viva voce*, predominated until the principles of objective testing could no longer be resisted. However, rather than following the psychometric approach slavishly, the long tradition of examiner assessment was not discarded. Instead, both the essay and the oral examination were retained in the 1975 Certificate of Proficiency in English revision, and three new papers which lent themselves to objective testing were introduced.

The instincts of the Cambridge ESOL team were vindicated later in the twentieth century when the psychometric approach was queried for emphasising reliability at the expense of validity. Validity as a concept means that what should be tested is tested. This seems a rather simplistic definition but those who stressed the need for valid forms of assessment maintained that objective testing involving multiple-choice could not predict, authentically, abilities such as writing and speaking, nor could it predict authentic listening skills unless the listening was based on real-time interaction. As the world of language testing caught up with the demands for communicative language use, so those who preferred objective testing and reliability had to cede to those who stressed that a reliable test was useless unless it was also valid. The new theory required that validity should be the first goal of assessment but accepted that reliability should not be ignored. It should be striven for as long as validity itself was not compromised.

This debate between psychometric-inclined testers of English and the Cambridge approach (a hybrid approach) still flourishes. As drafts of this chapter were being written in mid 2006, debate raged on the testing list subscribed to by professional testers throughout the world: LTEST-L@LISTS.PSU.EDU. The debate centred on the validity of direct tests if assessors were allowed to introduce a modicum of their own attitudes and beliefs into their rating. This use of judgement by assessors is a common problem even for distinguished testers who have been psychometrically trained and who, when contemplating individual judgements, shudder at what might have potential for unreliability in testing. Of course, there will always be some variation among assessors but the whole purpose of having clear criteria for them (usually in the form of descriptors which describe the level of language being used), which take out ambiguity and uncertainty, is to produce reliable levels of rating, provided that enough training and standardisation is provided for the assessors before they begin their work, and for all assessors regularly thereafter. I personally subscribe to a hybrid approach in which those tests lending themselves to objective assessment continue to be used, provided they are piloted and shown to be reliable, but I strongly favour direct tests of those skills (as opposed to knowledge) that do not lend themselves to the kinds of objective methods of testing characterised by multiple-choice questions, yes/no questions, true/false questions and filling in the gap questions, etc. If we use a multiple-choice method for testing writing, it is invalid, and no amount of extrapolation from the scores can address the question of whether that skill is being assessed validly. Therefore, we have to accept a small amount of variation in assessor assessment (a small degree of unreliability) in return for adherence to the over-riding concept of validity. Validity should always be the default position, not reliability. The existence of this dichotomy never fails to provoke those who are psychometrically inclined, for whom the god of reliability should not be sacrificed on the altar of validity.

The first comparative study of Cambridge's Proficiency examinations, specifically FCE, and the Educational Testing Service, Princeton's Test of English as a Foreign Language (TOEFL) examination was commissioned by John Reddaway, the Syndicate's Secretary, carried out by Professor Lyle Bachman and published in 1995. The major findings were that the two examinations came from differing philosophical perspectives and that, although the strengths of the Cambridge examination were clearly evident (the validity of the direct tests of speaking and writing), there were inconsistencies with regard to the equivalence of different tests offered on the same occasion (there were many varieties of the speaking test topics in order to prevent content leakage at test centres) and the reliability of the tests and assessors. The author stated that minor adjustments to the test development and trialling process could overcome these problems, thus increasing reliability through assessor training and more rigorous test trialling. These recommendations were carried out and rigorous test development was implemented by the creation within the EFL division of a new unit, the Evaluation Unit (later renamed the Research and Validation Group), established by the first Director of EFL/ESOL, Dr Peter Hargreaves.

All of the new EFL examinations which were introduced by Cambridge ESOL after 1975 adhere to the notion that validity is paramount but that it should also be supported by notions of reliability. In addition, two other concepts were embraced and became important in creating and developing examinations in English. They are *impact* and *practicality*. They consider how practical, useful and ethical an examination is. The twelve-hour 1913 version of the CPE would, nowadays, be regarded as impractical in terms of the amount of organisation and human resources which would be required to run the examinations in many countries with many examiners. The 1975 version reduced this time by a third, and by 1984 the revision process reduced the overall time to just under six hours, the time now commonly used, without reducing the effectiveness of the whole examination as a test of language proficiency.

In terms of *impact*, N. Saville describes this as: 'The influence of a test on general educational processes and on the individuals who are affected by the test results. It is recognised that examination boards like UCLES have a major impact on educational processes and on society in general because the examinations have widespread currency and recognition.'

The notion of *impact* further considers issues such as teachers teaching to the examination in spite of teaching syllabuses which may run contrary to the tests. It also includes *testing ethics* to which E. Shohamy has drawn attention. She comments on the power of examination boards, stating: 'Tests are powerful because they lead to momentous decisions affecting individuals and programs. They are conducted by authoritative and unquestioning judges who are backed by the language of science and numbers.'

The notion of *high-stake examinations* is also entailed in the ethical considerations noted by Shohamy in 'Language Testing: Impact' in the *Concise Encyclopaedia of Educational Linguistics*. Many of Cambridge's examinations are high-stake in the sense that momentous decisions, affecting candidates and their sponsors, are made by the authorities – decisions that can affect the lives of individuals in a major way. For example CPE results may affect whether or not a candidate is admitted to a university, as may results from the International English Language Testing Service (IELTS).

JACK ROACH – ADVOCATE OF THE CERTIFICATE OF PROFICIENCY IN ENGLISH AND THE DEVELOPMENT OF LINKS WITH THE BRITISH COUNCIL

Roach was an ardent advocate of EFL examinations who worked hard to build up the Certificate of Proficiency in English, particularly in Europe. He envisaged Cambridge playing a cultural and harmonious role in Europe and travelled extensively on the continent in the 1930s, producing useful and interesting papers which, for example, told of the rise of fascism and changing political alliances.

One of the links he cultivated, one which was to bear fruit over the next decades, was an agreement to co-operate with the recently created British Council, the British government's official arm for cultural and educational links with overseas countries. The first mention of the link, which soon involved Cambridge using British Council premises as local centres and their staff as local secretaries, particularly for EFL examinations, came in 1937. The link was formalised in a conference chaired by the Librarian of the Foreign and Commonwealth Office, Sir Stephen Gaselee, on 29 March 1941, which was attended by Roach and led by the then Secretary of the Syndicate, W. Nalder Williams. One example of this enduring link can be witnessed in the creation and maintenance of what would become the highly regarded English Language Testing Service (ELTS) – later IELTS – a high-stakes examination of English for academic and vocational purposes which is described more fully below. Roach left the Syndicate in 1945 for a post in the Civil Service Commission but he continued to have an interest in its work, particularly in EFL examinations. Many of his papers were unpublished but he eventually made them available to the Syndicate.

45 Jack Roach, Assistant Secretary from 1925 to 1945 (Cambridge Assessment)

46 EFL examination in Rome, 1956 (M/P 1/3)

THE DEVELOPMENT OF OTHER CAMBRIDGE
ENGLISH LANGUAGE EXAMINATIONS

Diploma in English Studies

One of the earlier English examinations was the Diploma in English Studies which was not unlike the early forms of the CPE, although it was much more difficult in terms of both language proficiency and literary skills. The Diploma was first offered in 1941, again not an auspicious time. By 1947, only 47 candidates had taken the examination in 11 countries, of whom 35 qualified for the award of the Diploma. By June 1982, the numbers had risen to only 203 from 21 countries, excluding the UK. Of these, only 74 were awarded Diplomas.

The Diploma was last offered in 1997. Four factors led to its abandonment. These were: the difficulty of the examination and consequent small candidature; the expense of administering it for such a small candidature in a large number of countries; the growing emphasis on language use in English examinations; and the growth of Departments of English in overseas countries which offered similar courses with local university examinations and certification.

The main suite of ESOL examinations

The main suite of general English proficiency examinations grew over time, particularly in the last two decades of the twentieth century. It began with the CPE in 1913 and was followed by the First Certificate in 1939 and the Diploma in English Studies in 1941.

Later additions to the main suite were mostly at the lower levels of proficiency where hundreds of thousands of students studied English and required some form of certification for work or other purposes. These two lower-proficiency additions were the Preliminary English Test (PET) and the Key English Test (KET), both based on the Council of Europe's work, within the Modern Languages Project during the 1970s and 1980s, to identify meaningful levels of functional competence (such as the Threshold and Waystage levels) and to specify learning objectives for teaching purposes. In the main suite, the Preliminary English Test comes below FCE at Threshold Level. It was introduced in 1980. It is described on Cambridge ESOL's webpage as 'an intermediate level exam, testing your ability to cope with everyday written and spoken communications'. The Key English Test is at the lowest level in the main suite and is described as 'an elementary level exam, testing your ability to deal with basic written and spoken communications' at Waystage Level. It was introduced in 1994.

However, not all developments were at the lower end of the proficiency spectrum. The Certificate in Advanced English (CAE) was developed for those who found the gap between FCE and CPE too large. This certificate is described on the Cambridge ESOL website as 'An advanced exam – if you can communicate with confidence in English for work or study purposes, this is the exam for you.' It was introduced in 1991.

Building on the Threshold and Waystage levels, the creation of the Council of Europe's Common European Framework of Reference for learning, teaching and assessment (1996) boosted Cambridge ESOL's exposure and applicability, as it allowed Cambridge's main suite of English examinations to fit into a common framework of reference within the European language teaching/learning context.

Other Cambridge ESOL examinations

During the 1990s, Cambridge ESOL developed other examinations in three distinct areas: modular skills-based assessment; Business and workplace English; and English for young learners. A new suite of skills-based assessment certificates has been developed recently in response to UK government policy to give structured support to the large number of immigrants and their families who have little or no English on arrival, and even long after arrival, in the UK.

Worldwide demands for Business English tests emerged in response to the growth of Business English programmes throughout the world as English became the lingua franca for millions of people working in business and commercial fields, and Human Resource managers, English teachers and course participants realised that neither general English coursebooks nor the tests from Cambridge's main suite were appropriate. Two sets of examinations are available: Business English Certificates (BEC), introduced in 1993, is a suite of three examinations designed to test English language ability used in the context of business; Business Language Testing Service (BULATS), introduced in 1998, is a multi-lingual assessment service for companies which require a rapid, accurate means of assessing language skills in English, French, German and Spanish.

A recent phenomenon in language teaching and testing has been the growth of programmes for young learners in Europe, Latin America and the Far East, as recently developed countries generated new, educated middle-class populations with aspiring parents who recognised that knowledge of English is one of the steps to advancement in the modern world. These programmes have developed separately from the English taught in state schools, and demands for tests for young learners were met by Cambridge ESOL's development of three levels of testing for children aged seven to twelve. The tests were introduced as recently as 1997 and are attracting increasing attention in state as well as private educational contexts.

In 2006, Cambridge ESOL's website www.cambridgeesol.org/index.htm claimed that they provide the world's leading range of certificates for learners of English. Each year they are taken by over 1.75 million people, in 135 countries.

Collaborative ESOL examinations

The International English Language Testing Service (IELTS)

One of the most successful collaborative ventures by Cambridge ESOL has been the development of the first English Language Testing Service (ELTS), originally in conjunction with the British Council and later, as IELTS, with the British Council and the International Development Program of Australian Universities and Colleges. The English Language Testing Service emerged out of the English Proficiency Test Battery. This was developed by Alan Davies of Edinburgh University, administered by the British Council overseas and used by tertiary institutions in the UK from 1966 to 1980 for admission to undergraduate and postgraduate degree programmes. It consisted mainly of objective tests.

Changing notions of the use and testing of language skills in context resulted in the validity of the English Proficiency Test Battery being questioned. As a result, a working party was set up in the mid 1970s to consider a new test, particularly one that would include the assessment of writing and speaking in the growing area of English for Specific Purposes. Thus, in 1980, after four years of development, the first version of ELTS was introduced with subtests linked to six academic areas of study (Life Sciences, Social Studies, Physical Sciences, Technology, Medicine, General Academic). The ELTS was innovative in its design and implementation but there were problems initially in the training and the maintenance of reliability of examiners. The problems with the first version of ELTS led to a revision process between 1986 and 1989, set up under the direction of Professor Charles Alderson of Lancaster University. British Council management support came from a team headed by Peter Hargreaves, who was at that time with the British Council. An Australian perspective was provided by Professor David Ingram of Griffith University who was seconded to the revision project in Lancaster from 1987, supported by the International Development Program of Australian Universities and Colleges.

After four years of development, administration of the first IELTS took place in 1989 when the six areas of study were reduced to three. By 1993, the candidature grew to reach over 30,000 and the test was available to candidates in 186 test centres in 105 countries. By then, Cambridge ESOL had developed an iterative programme of test revision, so another revision project was implemented from 1992 to 1995. The major change in 1995 involved the reduction of the three areas of study into two, the Academic variant and the General Training variant. The growth of applicants for vocational training, such as nurses, especially in Australia, revealed an area which demanded an appropriate test for immigration, work and continuing study purposes. A major research programme on the speaking and writing tests was implemented both in-house by Cambridge ESOL and by external consultants, managed by Cambridge ESOL. Funds have been provided by the International Development Program, Australia, since 1995, and by the British Council since 1998. These studies contributed a great deal to further IELTS revisions: the IELTS Speaking Revision Project (1998–2001) and the IELTS Writing Revision Project (2001–5).

IELTS has been extremely successful. It is managed jointly by Cambridge ESOL, the British Council and the International Development Program (IDP:IELTS), Australia. Growth in candidature has been rapid in recent years with significant demand for the examination in China as its economy and international trade has escalated. The number of candidates in 2006 worldwide was in excess of 700,000.

The International Legal English Certificate (ILEC)

The International Legal English Certificate is another collaborative venture. In response to requests for certification of the English of lawyers for whom English is not a first language, it is produced and assessed by Cambridge ESOL in collaboration with Translegal – Europe's leading firm of lawyer-linguists. It is recognised by leading associations of lawyers including the European Company Lawyers Association, the European Law Students Association,

47 IELTS in China, 2006 (photograph from British Council Beijing, provided by Sarah Deverell)

the International Association of Young Lawyers, and the European Young Bar Association.

International Legal English Certificate examinations centres exist in seventeen European countries and in Uruguay. It was launched in 2005 with the first test taking place in May 2006. If it progresses at the same rate as other new ESOL examinations, it will not take long for candidature to gain momentum and then increase rapidly. The development of this certificate is a good indicator of how flexibility has been built into Cambridge ESOL's response to demand – developing a new test without sacrificing integrity in the stages of development, administration and assessing.

RESEARCH AND INNOVATION

In 1988, A. Hughes *et al.*, in their *ELTS Validation Project Report*, claimed, in connection with the English Language Testing Service

Validation study, that the publication of detailed validation studies meets the criteria of public accountability. It was then that Cambridge ESOL began to produce research studies of validation and other concepts such as *reliability*, *impact* and *practicality*. The appointment of Dr Michael Milanovic in 1988 as head of what would become the Research and Validation Unit was a major innovation. It meant that all Cambridge ESOL examinations would be subject to the same rigorous processes in development and trialling as the psychometric tradition required. In addition, the Unit began researching the reliability of its tests of speaking and writing, and the methods of training and standardising assessors for the communicative skills of speaking and writing that were not reliant on the psychometric tradition.

Members of Cambridge ESOL now publish widely in academic journals specialising in testing and assessment. A series of research-based books in the Studies in Language Testing series (SiLT) has been created, with over twenty-five volumes produced since its inception in 1995. In addition to print-based publications, Cambridge ESOL's *Research Notes* are available on the web at www.cambridgeesol.org/rs_notes/index.cfm, as well as in hard copy, providing instant access to testing developments and news about changes to tests. They are an excellent way of spreading information to English language teachers and English language examiners (often the same people) about forthcoming developments, changes to examinations and trends and issues in English language testing, in an instantly accessible and timely format.

IT INNOVATIONS

The on-going series of *Research Notes* was one of the first IT-related publications. One of the latest appeared in 2007 when Cambridge ESOL published its first web-based report, *The IELTS Writing Assessment Revision Project: Towards a Revised Rating Scale* (by S. Shaw and P. Falvey), an account of the 2001–5 revision of the writing paper for IELTS. As the writing paper went 'live' at the beginning of 2005, it was decided that publication in hard copy would prevent examiners and teachers from gaining access to the detailed descriptions of the processes that took place during the revision project, and the rationale, research-based, for the changes that occurred.

Other chapters have described some of the innovations, often electronic, that are being implemented at Cambridge Assessment. One of the most important and valuable developments is electronic script management, which is being tested at the moment. It will allow an electronic version of a writing test answer script to be sent to Cambridge where the reliability of script grades awarded on site overseas can be checked and confirmed by return, instead of waiting for samples of scripts to be mailed or faxed to Cambridge.

Another IT innovation, one which is contentious, is interactive testing. A large bank of multiple-choice test items is used to gauge the level of a candidate's proficiency quickly and to provide the candidate with test items of an appropriate level of difficulty. For example the candidate is offered five items. On the completion of the five items, the interactive program selects another five items at a higher, at a lower or at the same level, depending on the candidate's scores. Once the next five items have been completed, the program again checks whether that level is appropriate and adjusts the next set of items until the candidate is operating at an appropriate level. In the context of examination boards providing interactive testing for their high-stakes examinations, much controversy has arisen because of the massive human resources required to produce an item bank sufficient to cover a large population of test-takers and to provide alternative items when candidates decide to re-take the test. For small, institutional organisations, interactive testing is a quick and reliable form of testing, but larger organisations find the logistics impossible. This is a good example of a useful innovation but one which fails the test of *practicality* for large testing organisations.

TEACHER AWARDS IN ESOL

Cambridge has always been involved in the training and standardisation of examination assessors, especially in the assessment of skills in writing and speaking. Its involvement in the field of English language teacher education qualifications has been relatively recent, with its language test for teachers, Cambridge Examination in English for Language Teachers (CEELT), launched in 1987. However, when the long-established teacher examinations of the Royal Society of Arts became at first a joint venture with, and subsequently subsumed under, Cambridge ESOL, the Cambridge Examination in English for Language Teachers was eventually phased out. The two qualifications which came from the Royal Society of Arts were the Certificate in English Language Teaching to Adults (CELTA), an initial qualification, and the Diploma in English Language Teaching to Adults (DELTA), which is aimed at those with substantial teaching experience who are seeking career progression. These have worldwide currency and are required for most applicants for teaching English in language schools in the UK and language schools elsewhere, especially in British Council teaching centres. The Diploma qualification can be gained either through full-time attendance at a course or through an in-service variety in which three organisations have collaborated: Cambridge ESOL, the British Council, and the well-known and respected language school and teacher training organisation International House.

As demand for more specialist qualifications has emerged, Cambridge ESOL has added four certificate-level examinations and one diploma-level examination to the two original qualifications. The four certificates include one that specialises in the growth area of English Language Teaching to Young Learners; an In-service Certificate in English Language Teaching which is equivalent to the Certificate in English Language Teaching to Adults full-time qualification; a certificate in teaching English in Further Education – a growth area serving those who teach English in the areas of Skills for Life, mainly for immigrants in the UK; and a Teacher Knowledge Test which differs from the other three new certificates in that it focuses on the core teaching knowledge needed by teachers of English – knowledge of language as opposed to knowledge of and skills for teaching language. Each of these certificates is a response to requests for qualifications or in response to perceived needs for such certificates.

The additional Diploma qualification is the International Diploma in Language Teaching Management (IDLTM). This qualification arose from the need for qualifications for teachers who move into lower and middle management in English Language Teaching and require skills other than teaching skills, such as Human Resource and financial management.

By 2006, overall candidature for all Cambridge's teacher awards was almost 12,000. An obvious spin-off for Cambridge ESOL is that much of the material used in their teacher awards requires knowledge of testing and assessment for ESOL examinations. This has a double effect. It provides lots of relevant material for the teacher training courses and for the teacher trainers. It also helps to develop awareness of Cambridge ESOL examinations among teachers. Another good feature of the Cambridge awards is the forging of a link between the curriculum and the examination, something which has always been true for the Cambridge examinations more generally. 'Teaching for the examination' was one of the criticisms of those who taught learners who took examinations based on psychometric principles. Cambridge ESOL wishes to make teachers much more informed about communicative teaching methods and learning concepts which they can illustrate through their direct tests of writing and speaking. It also helps teacher award candidates to become aware of the psychometric principles that inform Cambridge's indirect tests (e.g. language knowledge and reading comprehension tests), which lend themselves to objective scoring.

In many ways, an ideal situation has developed where the principles and methods of testing are merged with the principles and methods of teaching. One feature of the awards is that non-native speakers of English, those who speak English as a second or foreign language, can be participants on the teacher training courses as long as their language proficiency is at or near the level of an educated native speaker. This is an influential factor and gives the awards high levels of acceptability and credibility. One of the interesting features of native and non-native speakers of English is that, while the native speakers have good pronunciation and other good language skills, they are often weak in knowledge of how the language works – the grammar. Many of them are not graduates in English and have to learn or re-learn the grammar. Non-native speakers are much more likely to be graduates of English with a very good knowledge of English grammar.

THE MODERN ERA

Many thousands in the UK and in other countries worldwide have contributed to the development and growth of Cambridge ESOL examinations since 1913. The last quarter of a century, however, has seen significantly large growth in Cambridge personnel: examiners both in the UK and overseas for the direct tests of speaking and listening, and local secretaries who, appointed by Cambridge, operate at each centre throughout the world. They are responsible for all examinations arrangements, including the security of examination papers. Many local secretaries are based in British Council offices worldwide.

The modern era of expansion and growth arrived when John Reddaway, a Fellow of Emmanuel College, was appointed Secretary from 1983 to 1993. During his ten years in office he introduced many changes, including the secondment of two British Council officers as advisers from 1984 to 1990; the formal establishment of EFL as a division of the Syndicate in 1988; collaboration with the British Council to build a new British Council office in Tokyo; the merger of Royal Society of Arts examinations with Cambridge EFL examinations, also in 1988; and, most perspicaciously, identifying the emergence of China into the world, the opening of its markets and the opportunities for the growth of ESOL examinations. Reddaway oversaw the mergers, with Cambridge, of two boards: in 1999, the Association of Recognised English Language Schools (ARELS) which had offered language examinations since 1967 and, in 1993, the Oxford Delegacy which first offered English language examinations in 1978.

The examinations offered by those boards were eventually consolidated into Cambridge ESOL's Certificates in English Language Skills. This took place in 2002. Until Reddaway's tenure, even the fax was an innovation and there were no electronic databases to access – the telephone and the telex were the most used instruments of communication between a small ESOL staff at Cambridge and the rest of the world. By the time he ended his tenure as Secretary in 1993, Cambridge ESOL was well into the phase of rapid development, substantial growth and technological progress in communications and test development which we currently witness. Subsequent Secretaries have continued to support the modernisation and streamlining of ESOL developments, with the result that ESOL staff numbers in Cambridge now exceed 200 with thousands of examiners in over 135 countries.

Continuity in the Cambridge ESOL division was assured when Michael Milanovic was appointed in 2003 as Chief Executive of Cambridge ESOL, taking over after the untimely death of Peter

Hargreaves, who had overseen so many innovations and changes in processes in the division, including the professionalisation of assessment and testing for Cambridge examinations.

CONCLUSION

This account of slow, then steady, growth, followed by Cambridge ESOL's attention to the development and increase in expertise in language testing during the recent quarter of a century's rapid escalation of candidature for its ESOL examinations, appears to be an unbridled story of success. And, indeed, it is. Cambridge ESOL has every right to be congratulated on its professionalism. However, and there is always a 'however', a recent report by David Graddol, commissioned by the British Council, warns ESOL teachers and testers that the unparalleled growth and 'ownership' of English will, eventually, slow down to be replaced by a different scenario as individual countries develop their own institutions and their own forms of the English used by educated users in that country. Through its links with so many countries, its expertise in market intelligence and its informed insights, Cambridge ESOL should be in a good position to cope with these developments as they emerge.

6

RESEARCH AND DEVELOPMENT

GILLIAN COOKE

OVERVIEW

The introduction of Cambridge local examinations in 1858 was itself controversial, arousing interest and fuelling debate. A research rôle has always been integral to the work of Cambridge Assessment and without it the changes and adaptations which have been so readily embraced could not have taken place. But the rôle itself has taken many forms, from unstructured criticisms, projects and designated committees through to carefully constructed divisional plans.

At the time the Syndicate was set up, reliance on oral examinations as a means of testing candidates was waning. They had a strong tradition in the western world as being open and transparent but throughout the eighteenth century written answers were becoming more popular, offering greater impartiality, allowing the candidate more scope and time for expression and providing what many saw as a more uniform standard for measurement. Economically, oral examinations were costly to administer, unworkable for the new examination boards for whom 'local' was a key word, and by 1900 all candidates expected to sit essay-type examinations.

This development was not universally welcomed and a growing unease about the reliability of the essay examination led to experiments and investigations, initially in the USA, and pioneered by P. Hartog and E. Rhodes in the UK in the 1930s. Essay answers were subjected to scientific analysis to illustrate how examiners marked differently and, by the mid twentieth century, psychologists and statisticians began to be employed in the increasingly respected field of testing techniques.

The Educational Testing Service Unit was established in 1947 in the USA as a non-profit organisation devoted to research and measurement in education. It grew rapidly, gaining a strong reputation for its work in psychometric and intelligence testing and forcing assessment bodies worldwide to refine their testing strategies. By the mid 1960s scholastic aptitude tests were being developed in the UK, and objective-type tests were being trialled in the Syndicate's examinations in English for Foreign Students (English as a Foreign Language) and were later introduced in UK and overseas examinations. At the same time marking experiments were carried out involving double or triple marking techniques in attempts to reduce examiner inconsistencies.

Today, research includes studies in validity, reliability, comparability, consistency, standardisation, impact and practicability with the overall aim of improving assessment practices and making the process fairer. It also provides an opportunity to further knowledge in the field of assessment by publishing studies for scrutiny by academics and non-academics alike.

But, of course, this has not been the only impetus for research. The government became more involved in education as its importance for Britain's industrial success became more apparent. At first the boards' freedom was defended in many quarters. A report by the Royal Commission on Secondary Education in 1894 includes the comment that 'it would be difficult and undesirable . . . for a central authority . . . to prescribe in detail any uniform system' in the face of 'so many efficient and suitable agencies for examination'. But a uniform system did emerge during a century peppered with educational legislation. The GCSE, introduced in the 1980s, had, by 1994, become tightly regulated following the introduction of the National Curriculum, and Curriculum 2000 heralded the new A level.

The issues are complex and diverse, more so as we near the present and this chapter does not attempt to cover all the types of research work carried out over the past century and a half within the Syndicate. This brief, chronological overview, however, may give some insight into trends and developments faced by the Syndicate, together with some examples of how the board has responded.

THE BEGINNINGS OF RESEARCH

Was research born with the Syndicate in 1858? The early Syndicate minutes would suggest not. The self-assurance of the Syndics appears, by 21st-century standards, quite breathtaking. The examiners were chosen and appointed by the Syndics (at first, the Syndics were all examiners) and, their status assured, the need for the candidates to satisfy the examiners was everything. Complaints were generally dismissed and the topics of discussion at a conference of headmasters in 1873 concerned only an appeal for the Cambridge and Oxford boards to merge (as indeed happened 120 years later) and a request that the boards introduce examinations for younger boys.

There was some discussion about standards, however, and in 1873 a simple entry in the Syndicate minutes records that the Syndics decided to raise the standard for Junior Arithmetic and lower it for Junior English Literature.

As the examinations expanded, the need to recruit more examiners became more pressing and the integrity of the examiners began to give some cause for concern. In 1874, a Presiding Examiner was questioned about giving a Saturday paper on a Friday and, in 1875, a French examiner was accused of 'allowing a stranger to look over some of the answers entrusted to him'. If guilty, both were to be dismissed. In June 1885, Dr Reid, a Syndic at the time, questioned the work of examiners and proposed that committees be appointed to revise their work. Dr Reid was asked to draft suggestions with the help of the Secretary, G. F. Browne, but it is not clear that these were ever carried out. Certainly Dr Reid's tenure ended shortly afterwards.

Outside the Local Examinations Syndicate extensive questions were being asked about the new school examination process. Henry Latham, a tutor at Trinity Hall in the 1870s, argued for the importance of examinations in allowing the candidate to demonstrate a skill, rather than as a medium to convey knowledge. Latham drew extensively on his familiarity with educational assessment overseas and with university and civil service examinations to ask searching questions about reliability of examinations. In John Roach's view in *Public Examinations in England, 1850–1900*, Latham raised the issue of psychology in examinations 'when experimental psychology hardly existed'. In the late 1880s the subject of examinations again came under scrutiny after the publication of a petition with 400 signatories claiming that examinations produced 'overstrain' in candidates. The debate which followed led, ultimately, to the Education Act of 1902, but, in terms of a thorough analysis of the examination system, the leading contribution was made by F. Y. Edgeworth. He conducted studies on the consistency of marking, looked at different examiners and examiners' marking over consecutive years, and wrote popular accounts of his work in the *Journal of Education* in the late 1880s.

Neville Keynes, Secretary of the Syndicate and Browne's successor, recorded comments he received on examinations and kept news cuttings from the *Journal of Education*. By the 1890s, the Oxford Delegacy of Local Examinations and the Local Examinations Syndicate had been examining long enough to be confronted by 'comparability' issues. In December 1891, the York Boys' Local Secretary explained that they were switching to the Oxford Locals because 'their papers are more even, contain fewer traps and catchy questions and the questions are confined more strictly to the limits of the syllabus'. Keynes also collected comments about standards. Mr Beaver in 1892 wrote: 'I think that almost uniformly the senior papers throughout this examination were proportionately easier than those for the Juniors.' As the earliest studies of comparability over time, these comments are notable for their concern that standards were *rising*. Keynes collected comments year on year throughout the 1890s on this issue, and one Presiding Examiner explains his own study as follows: 'For nine years out of the last ten it has been my habit to do the Junior Arithmetic paper at racing pace and my average time is just under 40 minutes . . . last year's I did in 24 – this year's took just an hour.'

The issue of 'overstrain' was taken up by the *Journal of Education* in 1893. In an article on examination timetables of the various examination boards it was pointed out that, despite slight improvements, the timetables of the Cambridge board 'are still far in excess of what any prudent physician or hygienist would sanction', citing as 'indefensible' the Junior practical examination in Chemistry or Botany which was timetabled 'from 6 to 8 at night'.

I N consequence of the discussion which took place three
years ago in the *Times,* and the strong comments of the
press on the Cambridge University Local Examinations, a
slight improvement has been made in the time-tables, but
they are still far in excess of what any prudent physician or
hygienist would sanction. We have before us the time-table
for the examination which is just over, and find that by it
a Junior—that is, a boy or a girl of fifteen years or under—
may have seven-and-a-half hours of paper work in one day,
and, what is equally indefensible, may have to undergo a
practical examination in chemistry or botany from 6 to 8
at night. We know from experience what the official answer
to such complaints is sure to be : The examination *must*
not extend beyond five days and a half, and it *must* include
some twenty different subjects. In other words, the Syndicate say : The problem we set ourselves is to get a quart into
a pint pot, and we manage it with as little pressure and as
little spilling as is possible. The obvious retort is : Why not
give up what, on your own showing, is an impossible problem ?
But we would venture to remind the Syndicate that the
University of London examinations, which are generally
criticised for embracing too many, not too few, subjects,
never extend beyond a week, and never are prolonged into
the night hours.

48 Cutting from the *Journal of Education* 1893 concerning the dangers to
health of examination timetables (PP/JNK 2/2)

So how did the Syndicate react to the criticisms and justify its
position? Although Keynes kept or copied comments for retention,
the Syndicate minutes reveal that criticisms were discussed but, as
often, rejected. Certainly the examination reports do not dwell on
these issues, preferring to make comparisons about the quality of
answers rather than the questions, although the Elementary Algebra
examination for Juniors in 1893 is acknowledged as being 'slightly'
more difficult than for the previous year and there were no more science practical examinations for Juniors beginning at 6 p.m. after 1893!

By the 1890s, criticism of school examinations focused more on
the need to improve the system – as argued by Edgeworth – than to
abolish it, and Keynes collected articles from the *Journal of Education* which published detailed dissections of particular question
papers and provided a useful forum for a lively exchange of views.
The Head Masters' and Head Mistresses' Conferences provided an

equally important forum for discussion between examination boards and teachers, while the Syndicate minutes show that, although specific complaints may have been rejected, the Syndicate was fully occupied with the business of refining and developing syllabuses.

The standard of examinations may have been a subject for debate, but the calibre of examiners at the Syndicate in the nineteenth century remained largely unchallenged. The list of examiners in 1900 shows that almost all were Cambridge graduates or Fellows of colleges, and most were clergymen. The applications were brief and included no reference to teaching experience. Scrutiny, beyond the occasional observation that an elderly examiner had become 'fussy and troublesome' or hard of hearing, was rare.

Gradually, external comments and opinions began to penetrate the confidence of the Syndics and concessions were made, or at least recorded. In 1901, the Syndicate agreed to simplify the 'teaching of French syntax' to appease the French Minister of Public Instruction, and it also decided to seek teachers' opinions as to the value of the Syndicate's subject reports. Various committees began to be set up to consider regulations and syllabuses for particular subjects and the subject committees began to evolve, growing to become a significant forum for discussion and syllabus development by the mid twentieth century.

In 1906, the newly created Board of Education asked the Syndicate 'for samples of work and marked papers written by Senior Candidates together with schedules of marks obtained and information as to the principles of marking and actual percentages adopted'. The Syndicate replied after long discussion and with tangible caution: yes, they would forward the papers to Whitehall but 'they would prefer that the investigation should take place at Cambridge'.

Eight years later, the Board of Education turned the screw. In its Proposals for Examinations dated July 1914, it outlined plans for new examinations and included the statement that, from an unspecified date, 'no schools recognised for grants from the Board of Education will be able to take the Preliminary, Junior or Senior Examinations as offered by the Cambridge or Oxford Local Examinations'. The Syndicate agreed to confer with the Oxford Delegates before replying. In November 1915, the University of Cambridge released a memo outlining the two new examinations that 'The Syndicate have decided to establish', the School Certificate and the Higher School Certificate.

NATIONAL EXAMINATIONS

In 1918 the School Certificate and Higher School Certificate were introduced nationally. These were group certificate examinations and required candidates to pass in a range of subjects. From the outset they were not particularly popular and the methods employed by the examination boards began to be scrutinised more closely. In 1918 the Syndicate's Joint Committee for Examinations was set up to monitor progress of the new examinations. Committee members included representatives from teaching associations and the minutes reveal that free and open discussions on particular question papers took place throughout the 1920s.

In 1931 the Syndics were asked to co-operate with the Board of Education over a proposed investigation into the July School Certificate Examination. After initial acceptance, the Syndics sent a rather feeble request that the investigation be 'deferred to some later date' 'in the interests of National Economy', but this was refused and the investigation was carried out. Although the formalities were not unpleasant, the results were clearly imposed on the Cambridge Syndics: that a certain minimum standard in English composition be accepted and that the Syndicate accept a 'slightly lower standard' in any two languages for a Group II pass. The following year Sir Philip Hartog asked if he could carry out an investigation of the School Certificate on behalf of the Carnegie Examinations Enquiry (part of the Educational Testing Service). He was turned down by 'a courteous letter stating that the Syndicate could not accede to the request'.

But Sir Philip Hartog and others who criticised the School Certificate and Higher School Certificate group system would not go away. Hartog demonstrated shortcomings in the methods of marking which he believed were flawed with inconsistencies. He questioned in particular the validity, consistency and usefulness to employers of examinations and was vociferous in his criticism of the School Certificate system. In his speech to the National Union of Teachers (NUT) in 1937, he argued against a system that forced examining bodies 'into the farce of passing large numbers of candidates, incompetent in particular subjects, in order to avoid the tragedy of ploughing [failing] them'.

By this time the Syndicate had set up an internal Research Committee to carry out specific projects and experiments. In 1937 the committee considered a scheme for objective tests in science, to look at factual knowledge, reasoning power and capacity for presentation. Two larger projects were also considered, one on oral examinations and the other on English composition.

Jack Roach, Assistant Secretary, had written *Some Problems of Oral Examinations in Modern Languages* in the late 1920s and this was reprinted and circulated as a joint piece of work by the Syndicate and the British Council in 1945. Roach had been appointed in 1925 and had worked hard to expand the new Certificate of Proficiency in English examination, which, despite a promising start, had struggled to survive the First World War. A modern linguist, Roach championed the methods of modern language learning that are taken for granted today and he had argued successfully for the Phonetics paper to be dropped from the examination in 1932. In his work on oral examinations, he addressed the difficulties in testing standards consistently in this method of examining, highlighting those issues which were more difficult to measure in oral than written examinations. He placed strong emphasis on validity and consistency, and raised many concerns about the human frailties of examiners that have enduring relevance, matters covered in greater detail in chapter 5.

The English Composition Experiment was 'designed to investigate the degree of reliance . . . placed on the marks of the examiners in what is admittedly one of the most difficult subjects to assess numerically' and takes up a theme which was aired by Hartog at the conference of the National Union of Teachers. The first parts aimed to measure consistency of marking by five examiners and the final part was designed to check conformation to the standard as laid down by the Chief Examiner. The experiment was a major piece of work for the Syndicate, involving the marking and re-marking of 400 scripts and, despite interruption from the Second World War, a report on the experiment was finally published in 1946. In his report, Dr J. Wishart of the Statistical Laboratory (a Syndic) acknowledged that composition marks were liable to large errors, but recognised that improvements could readily be made and some had been introduced as early as 1940. The Research Committee welcomed the report but Joseph Brereton, then Assistant Secretary, was concerned about the relevance and accessibility of the work and asked how it could be 'turned into a more popular account of the experiment' – a comment which certainly strikes a chord today.

Emboldened, the Research Committee set up a research fund in 1946 of £750 p.a. for three years. Brereton became Secretary of the Syndicate and applied to the newly formed National Foundation for Educational Research for Corporate membership. The following year a joint committee was set up with the British Council and University of London Institute of Education to investigate English language tests overseas.

Throughout the 1940s the number of Syndicate committees proliferated and, as well as a re-constituted Research Committee, there were Examiners' Committees, imposing strict and detailed instructions for marking, and a Special Committee on Examination Reform. This latter committee discussed the proposals put forward for the new GCE examination, including the Norwood Committee's recommendations described in chapter 3. In these discussions there was close and regular consultation between the examination boards. In *The Case for Examinations* written in 1944, Brereton highlighted some of the issues faced by the boards and, while he was 'horrified' at the enduring Victorian stereotype of the question papers, he warned against the boards developing over-detailed syllabuses, excluding teachers and failing to monitor examiners.

The introduction of the General Certificate of Education in 1951 provided the examination boards with a new challenge regarding standards, and in 1953 and 1956 the Syndicate took part in joint consultations with other boards to check the co-ordination of pass standards at Ordinary and Advanced levels. Standardisation was a prominent issue and the initial concerns seem to have focused on rising pass standards. However, by 1954 the Syndicate was forced to respond to claims of falling standards (or rising results) and explained it in part by candidates dropping weaker subjects. Standardisation remained another prominent theme and in 1969 the Syndicate published a candid report

49 Joseph Lloyd Brereton, Secretary from 1945 to 1961 (Cambridge Assessment)

on standards at GCE O level based on a survey conducted among its centres. The report reluctantly concludes that there was 'much disparity' between expectations of schools and the awarded results.

The work of the Educational Testing Service (ETS) in Princeton, USA, aroused considerable interest during the 1950s, and visitors from the Syndicate returned with glowing reports and inspiration to try out innovative techniques. For example, in 1950 the examinations for English as a Foreign Language (EFL) adopted the Educational Testing Service model of randomising script allocation prior to sending them out to examiners, continuing its tradition of engaging in independent and innovative research for English language examinations. The Educational Testing Service stretched, of course, beyond EFL, but it was competition with other EFL examinations which gave a strong impetus to the Syndicate to develop its research activities, as is illustrated in the chapter on English language examinations.

A COLLABORATIVE RESEARCH UNIT

The benefits of collaborative research work with other boards had long been appreciated but were taken a step further in the board's response to a Report of the Working Party on the Schools' Curricula and Examinations in 1964 which advocated the need for co-operation in the field of research. Initially an inter-board conference on research projects was suggested, but in December 1966 the first meeting of a proposed test development and research unit was held between representatives of the Syndicate, the Oxford and Cambridge Schools Examination Board (OCSEB), the University of Oxford Delegacy of Local Examinations (UODLE) and the Joint Matriculation Board (JMB). The functions and staffing arrangements were outlined at this meeting and funding was discussed. The Educational Testing Service was held as the model for the Unit, to the extent that it was proposed to send the new director of the Unit, when appointed, to Princeton for training before it was built up.

In 1967 the Joint Matriculation Board pulled out of the joint venture, deciding to set up its own research unit, and the three other boards formally set up the Test Development and Research Unit with a contribution from each board of £10,000. Particular care was taken to ensure that all the boards had an equal stake. The financial pooling of resources was a major attraction in the setting up of the Unit but it became an administrative burden and a source of resentment in later years and was ultimately cited as a contributing factor to the Unit's demise in 1985.

The Unit was situated in Cambridge to enable it to use a Syndicate IBM computer, but it was placed under the constitution of the Oxford and Cambridge Board for simplicity. A lease was initially taken on 11 Station Road in Cambridge. Then, in 1972, it moved to Drosier House, also in Cambridge. David Shoesmith was appointed as Director in March 1968 and he reported to the management committee

50 Drosier House, Harvey Road, Cambridge, 2007. Former offices of the Test Development and Research Unit (photograph by Nigel Luckhurst)

consisting of the four Secretaries (there were two for the Oxford and Cambridge Board) and two academic representatives from each of the three boards. The initial aim of the Unit was 'to investigate and develop methods of examining alternative or ancillary to the traditional ones and also to conduct research in the wider field of examinations'. The Unit's staff produced a series of specific research reports each year and the Director published a report to the management committee annually, which summarised the year's work.

The influence of the Test Development and Research Unit, under the guidance of David Shoesmith, grew steadily. The 1973 Annual Report of the Syndicate acknowledged that staff of the Unit were making a 'valuable contribution' to the discussions on the development of a common syllabus for the proposed 16 plus examination and the need for 'different depths of treatment for different ability ranges'. Throughout the early 1970s the Unit was engaged increasingly in multiple-choice test development, item writing and pre-testing and, in 1974, all of the Syndicate's multiple-choice test development work was transferred to it. It also had a separate function as a research unit, and conducted a variety of projects independently and with other examination boards. It was able to engage in inter-board research from a unique position of having access to scripts and syllabuses from three examination boards. From this position it was also an attractive project partner for other boards' research departments and Shoesmith served as a representative of the GCE boards on the Forum on Comparability set up by the Schools Council.

The Unit, however, did not have exclusive rights to carry out research, and other research projects and collaborative developments took place during this period. In 1972, for example, the Standing Research Advisory Committee consisting of Officers of GCE boards was set up to deal with matters of common interest, including comparability of standards. In 1975, at the request of the British Council, the Syndicate began developing an English Language Testing Service to assess the competence in English of non-native English students studying courses in English-speaking countries. Another independent project, the Assessment of Graded Objectives, was launched at the end of 1982 under the direction of Robert Tuffnell, which carried out a large-scale survey of the views of schools, local education authorities, teachers' organisations and inspectors with the help of the Test Development and Research Unit. Although GCSE was still a few years away, the 16+ examination, an alternative to the GCE O level and Certificate of Secondary Education, had been introduced in some subjects and graded objectives were significant in tackling problems associated with this examination which took in a wide ability range.

Throughout the 1970s the examination boards were under increasing pressure to justify their position as experts in the field of assessment by being pro-active in research. The Syndicate was heavily engaged in research work generated by the Schools Council papers on the development of a new sixth-form curriculum, and Tom Wyatt, the Secretary, wrote of the board being on a 'tenuous tightrope' between accusations of dictating what should be taught by teachers and responding to 'contemporary developments'. The pressure was felt by all examination boards and this seeming inability to please all critics is addressed succinctly by A. Robin Davies of the Oxford and Cambridge Board in his introduction to Bardell, Forrest and

Shoesmith's *Comparability in GCE: A Review of the Boards' Studies, 1964–1977*: 'If we merely state that comparability exercises are regularly conducted and do not show our hand, we appear to have something to hide. If we try to explain them, their complexities and limitations invite misunderstanding and misinterpretation. On balance, the preferable alternative seemed to be to "publish and be damned". We have, and probably shall be.'

By 1976 the Test Development and Research Unit with its new computerised item-banking system was described as 'the largest test development agency of its kind in the country'. Despite this acclaim, the Unit itself continued to be dogged by financial uncertainties. David Shoesmith's initial contract was for three years and throughout the 1970s he made repeated applications to the three controlling boards for contract renewals, more funding, larger premises and more staffing.

As the Syndicate grew in size compared with the Oxford and Cambridge Board and the Oxford Delegacy, the proportion of Test Development and Research Unit work required for the Syndicate began to overshadow the work required by the other examination boards. In addition to having a greater share of the UK market, the Syndicate also carried out a substantial number of examinations overseas, which were increasingly being tailored to particular countries' requirements. This created an imbalance of research work between the boards, which was aggravated further in 1979 by the formation of the Cambridge, Oxford and Southern School Examinations Council (COSSEC), a consortium of examination boards. This became the new controlling body for the Test Development and Research Unit and originally included the Oxford Delegacy as well as the other three boards, but the Oxford Delegacy pulled out. Initially David Shoesmith predicted that the Test Development and Research Unit could survive without Oxford Delegacy funding, but it soon became apparent that the financial burden this placed on the Oxford and Cambridge Board, which commissioned very little work, made it uneconomic for the Test Development and Research Unit to continue in its existing form.

In 1983 David Shoesmith highlighted other problems, such as the increasing divergence of the functions of test development and research. Test development, he argued, had become a 'manufacturing'

process, producing around 100 tests a year, while research was conducted at a much slower and incompatible pace. The independent
status of the Test Development and Research Unit, once upheld as a
strength, had begun to have an adverse effect on staff working relationships within the participating boards. In 1985 it was wound up,
but Shoesmith continued to advise the Syndicate on the Research
Advisory Committee, and many of the Unit's staff transferred to
the employment of the Syndicate or the Oxford and Cambridge
Board.

DIVERSIFICATION

By the end of 1985, a new forum for research had been established
within the Council for Examination Development under the leadership of Ron McLone. The Council was charged with maintaining
contact, both inside and outside the examination boards, in respect of
the need for changes and innovations. It included representatives of
the teaching profession, local education administration, further and
higher education and industry and commerce.

The Council for Examination Development pioneered many new
tests and examinations in the 1980s in a period notable for its diversification. The foundations were laid for Information Technology (IT)
experimentation in the Cambridge Information Technology Examinations and Computer Enhanced Design and Realisation Project.
Critical thinking examinations were initiated in the Thinking Skills
Tests and vocational examinations were developed in the Technical, Vocational and Educational Initiative and the Law Studies Test.
There were also projects involving collaboration with local education authorities, such as the Records of Achievement Project and the
modular A level, which made its debut in 1989.

During the 1980s, however, research continued to be conducted in
other divisions of the Syndicate: the government's announcement in
1984 that the General Certificate of Secondary Education (GCSE)
would replace GCE O level and CSE examinations in 1988 generated more research and syllabus development work for the Midland
Examining Group, to which the Syndicate belonged. The Midland
Examining Group set up four research projects under the auspices

of each of its offices, all of which published reports on coursework from the centres' and candidates' point of view, modular aggregation, coursework moderation and differentiation. One of the new inter-board GCSE committees, the Inter-Group Research Committee, carried out the first GCSE comparability studies on the 1988 and 1989 examinations. The Joint Council subsequently took on the research remit from the GCE and GCSE Secretaries.

Although in 1988 one third of Syndicate business was concerned with GCSE, preparations were already advancing for the introduction of an international version of the new examination, initially called the International Certificate of Education, but introduced in 1989 as the International General Certificate of Secondary Education (IGCSE). The Syndicate had also recently developed a new international examination for Singapore called the N level, which was examined for the first time in autumn 1984. Government regulation may not have had a direct impact on these international examinations but research was necessary for the board to maintain credibility in a competitive marketplace. In the area of English as a Foreign Language, the Syndicate was engaged in a series of objective, subjective, oral and aural tests, and commissioned research to counter accusations from competitors that the Syndicate carried out too little research to ensure 'a reliable and valid standard', particularly regarding the assessment of essays. To support the English Language Testing Service, for example, the Rapid Access Management Information System was introduced to make test scores and candidate details readily accessible for validation studies.

The diversification of research work in the 1980s was arguably a result of increased governmental pressure on the boards. With GCSE and IGCSE in infancy, the future was far from certain and new types of examinations provided some insurance cover in an increasingly political arena. Although the Syndicate was applying its research expertise in other areas of assessment, many in the organisation (notably the Secretary, John Reddaway) felt the need to replace the Test Development and Research Unit with a specific new research facility dedicated to pure research with a broad perspective. The pressure from within was mirrored by that from the UK regulator and overseas ministries, which needed the Syndicate to generate original research, establish quality controls and satisfy demands for account-ability, while the Syndicate was also keen to promote its 'expertise in educational measurement' to generate revenue. A Research Advisory Committee was therefore set up in 1987 and Dr Robert Wood was asked to carry out an extensive survey of research in assessment. His publication, *Assessment and Testing*, is far-reaching. In it he high-lights the importance of validity and berates the examination boards for not giving it precedence over reliability studies. His study goes well beyond the scope of the Syndicate and it led to the establishment of a new research division, called the Research and Evaluation Division (RED), which was set up in 1994, under a new director, Alastair Pollitt.

A DESIGNATED RESEARCH DIVISION

The new Research and Evaluation Division, like the Test Development and Research Unit twenty years before, did not have a monopoly on research carried out within the Syndicate. The English as a Foreign Language Division, in particular, continued to pioneer its own research. In 1989 the division itself was restructured, with a new director and a strong and independent research team, which forged and strengthened partnerships with, among others, the RSA, the British Council and the English Language Testing Service and built a solid reputation for its research capabilities.

Another similarity with the Test Development and Research Unit was the new research division's physical separation from the rest of the organisation, housed first in Lloyds House, then in Furness Lodge, both in Cambridge. Unlike the Test Development and Research Unit, however, the Research and Evaluation Division was controlled solely by the Syndicate. It was to provide a research innovation, evaluation and development service to support all parts of the Syndicate. Staff in the division initially covered new and existing areas of research through the Inter-Board Group, the Measurement and Psychology Section and the Evaluation Service. Work included inter-board research and studies in cognitive psychology, which looked at the psychometric properties of examination questions. Staff were also involved in the training of examiners in question writing skills and in

51 Awarding Meeting for the Singaporean N level Examination, 2007
(photograph by Nigel Luckhurst)

supporting awarding procedures. The division expanded during the
1990s and new units were created within it. The National Curriculum
Group was set up on a contractual basis with government agencies for
the development of national curriculum tests at primary level. The
Information Technology in Assessment and Learning Unit was created to advise on the role of IT in the Syndicate Group's professional
activities.

One of the dominant themes for the new research division was
comparability, both between boards and over time, and a large proportion of studies published during this time were on comparability.
Longitudinal studies looking at standards over time were given a new
impetus in the 1990s by a small but consistent upward trend in examination results. Concerns about comparability were also raised at internal committees and the subject became an area of increasing interest
for the media. The government regulatory body published a report of
studies on public examinations over time, covering the period 1975 to
1995. After discovering a paucity of material to carry out such research

effectively, the School Curriculum and Assessment Authority set up
a national archive in 1996 which required all awarding bodies to send
agreed samples of scripts, question papers, syllabuses and marking
schemes to be used to conduct five-yearly reviews of standards. The
boards also instigated their own studies as a form of 'self regulation',
either as independent or inter-board studies. In 1995, for example,
the GCE boards published a study commissioned from the Curriculum, Evaluation and Measurement Centre on comparability between
boards, which included data from 1991, 1992 and 1993. During this
period, research staff were engaged in a variety of work which involved
technical expertise such as the analysis of data and provision of technical advice to other Syndicate staff.

As well as conducting its own research, the Syndicate contributed
to a range of independent, inter-board and international studies from
its new research division. Local authorities generated work on gender
differences, for example, and international studies focused on the performance of pupils of the same age in the same subject from a range of
different countries. A study on 'prior attainment' was carried out on
the introduction of Curriculum 2000, the new A and AS level examination. Candidate level data were matched across boards and years
so that prior GCSE achievement could be used as an indicator of the
calibre of candidates entering for the new AS and A levels.

Research projects were also generated by new government regulations. The School Examinations and Assessment Council's code of
practice for GCSE examinations initiated studies into new GCSE
subjects such as the syllabus in Combined Sciences, which became
a popular alternative to single science subject examinations. The
Midland Examining Group developed a series of new syllabuses
for 1998, many based on existing projects such as the School
Mathematics Project and the Schools History Project. Other syllabuses included the Avery Hill and Bristol Project for Geography and the Salter's, Nuffield and Suffolk Science syllabuses which
introduced more options and greater diversification in mainstream
examinations.

A significant part of the research division's work was the collection
and analysis of statistical data, including the annual publication of
statistical data at results time. In 1988, the UK examining boards

collaborated to produce a comprehensive set of inter-board statistics which are published annually. The impact of increased technology has been felt most acutely on the use of statistics and has revolutionised studies involving statistical analysis. Integrated data sets that include statistics from all the boards, yet can also be broken down to candidate level, can now be created.

The Research and Evaluation Division remained intact when the Syndicate restructured into business streams in 1998, and subsequently worked with staff in each of the divisions of OCR, Cambridge International Examinations and Cambridge ESOL. In 2002 the division itself was restructured and the Assessment Directorate was formed under Ron McLone. The Assessment Directorate proved to be a transitional experience for the research staff, and the Assessment, Research and Development Division was established in 2006 under a new director, Tim Oates. It encompasses four broad areas covering New Developments, Psychometrics, Research and Outreach in the form of the Cambridge Assessment Network. The new division continues to conduct some of the work initiated by the Research and Evaluation Division and the Assessment Directorate, but there have also been changes. The emphasis is shifting away from comparability studies, particularly inter-board studies, although a project on comparability over time was completed in 2003. The focus for cognitive psychology research is shifting too and moving away from the candidate towards the examiner.

Arguably, assessment bodies have been hesitant in grasping the potential for technological application in assessment, but technology now plays a leading role in the development of contemporary research techniques. On-screen marking is emerging and the potential to study a wide selection of item-level data from a candidate is becoming a reality. Electronic marking techniques provide Cambridge Assessment with an opportunity to manipulate groupings and monitor marking in real time thus allowing research into marking to be carried out at levels that were unimaginable fifty years ago. Unprecedented research into marking techniques is itself driven by technological development as the data collected can be fed into the new processes of automated marking systems. The Internet provides wider access to a varied and worldwide research network while raising the challenge for research staff to compete and share studies on a worldwide scale by publishing widely in an informed and accurate way.

Research staff are also instrumental in the development of other new breeds of examinations, such as the collaborative ventures of Achieve for Key Stage 2 and 3 Maths, English and Science, and UNI test, a university entrance examination. BMAT, a Biomedical Admissions Test, was introduced to eighty countries through the Assessment Directorate in November 2005.

CONCLUSION

It is not easy to summarise the problems, achievements and challenges experienced by those involved in research and development work over the past 150 years. The earliest comments and investigations may appear crude set against more recent initiatives, but staff since 1858 have all fed ideas into the melting pot and the result is a rich legacy that is greater than the sum of its parts. Research has become more transparent, more accessible and arguably more political. It has also diversified and adapted to new areas and initiatives. Research at Cambridge Assessment may have had a faltering start but will undoubtedly continue as an integral and essential part of the organisation.

APPENDIX I
CHRONOLOGY

1857	Syndics appointed by the University's Council of the Senate
1858	Examinations Syndicate formally established in February. First examinations held in December
1864	First examinations overseas – six senior candidates in Trinidad
1865	First female candidates accepted for an initial trial period of three years
1869–1922	Higher Local Examinations held
1878	Syndicate amalgamated with Local Lectures Syndicate
1886	Staff moved to Syndicate Buildings in Mill Lane
1895–1920	Preliminary Examinations held (to 1939 for overseas examinations)
1913	Certificate of Proficiency in English introduced in December
1917	Secondary School Examinations Council established
1918	Introduction of School Certificate and Higher School Certificate
1918	UCLES Joint Committee for Examinations formed
1923	Senior Local Examination became the School Certificate for UCLES
1939	Junior Examination discontinued (continued overseas until 1953)
1939	Lower Certificate in English introduced
1941–97	Diploma in English Studies
1941	Collaborative agreement signed with the British Council (March) and the Joint Council formed
1943	Publication of Norwood Report on Curriculum and Examinations in Secondary Schools, produced by committee chaired by Sir Cyril Norwood and including W. Nalder Williams. Led to GCE examinations and UCLES School Examinations Committee

1944	UCLES School Examinations Committee replaced Joint Committee for Examinations
1945	UCLES Awarding Committee for Overseas Examinations set up
1951	Introduction of GCE examinations
1952–80	Special examinations for members of HM Forces
1964	West African Examinations Council established in the first localisation
1964	Secondary School Examinations Council replaced by Schools Council
1965	UCLES moved to New Syndicate Buildings, 1 Hills Road
1965	Introduction of Certificate of Secondary Education
1968–85	Test Development and Research Unit
1970	Sir Ivor Jennings Building opened at Syndicate Buildings
1975	Lower Certificate in English became First Certificate in English
1975	CPE examination revised
1979	Cambridge Oxford and Southern School Examinations Council established
1982	UCLES Council for Home Examinations replaced School Examinations Committee
1983–94	UCLES Council for Examination Development
1983–98	UCLES Council for International Examinations
1984	Schools Council replaced by Secondary Examinations Council
1984	CPE examination revised
1985–98	Midland Examining Group administered GCSE examinations
1985	Frank Wild Building opened at Syndicate Buildings
1988	School Examinations and Assessment Council formed from Secondary Examinations Council
1988	First GCSE examinations
1988	First UCLES A level Modular Bank System examinations
1989	Introduction of Advanced Supplementary (AS) examinations
1990	English Language Testing Service re-launched as International English Language Testing Service
1990	Southern Universities Joint Board agreed to merge with UCLES
1991	Report of the Review Committee of the Syndicate regarding future development
1992	UCLES gained the Queen's Award for Export Achievement

1993	School Curriculum and Assessment Authority formed from School Examinations and Assessment Council and National Curriculum Council
1993	East Midlands Regional Examinations Board (CSE board) merged with UCLES
1994	GCSE code of practice becomes statutory
1995–8	Oxford and Cambridge Examinations and Assessment Council administered GCE A level examinations
1995	Oxford and Cambridge Schools Examination Board merged with UCLES
1995	University of Oxford Delegacy of Local Examinations merged with UCLES
1995	GCE A/AS level code of practice introduced by School Curriculum and Assessment Authority
1996	Acquisition of Oxford Association of Recognised Language Schools examinations
1997	School Curriculum and Assessment Authority merged with National Council for Vocational Qualifications to form Qualifications and Curriculum Authority
1998	Creation of Oxford Cambridge and RSA Examinations (OCR)
1998	Creation of International Examinations, later University of Cambridge International Examinations (CIE)
1998	Creation of Cambridge EFL which in 2002 became Cambridge ESOL
1998	Regent Street Building opened by the Chancellor, HRH the Duke of Edinburgh
2001	First AS examinations from Curriculum 2000
2005	9 Hills Road offices opened in March by the Vice-Chancellor, Professor Alison Richard
2005	University of Cambridge Local Examinations Syndicate renamed Cambridge Assessment for all but legal purposes

APPENDIX 2
SECRETARIES OF THE SYNDICATE

Bibliography

UNPRINTED SOURCES

Cambridge Assessment Archives

Acc. 3007	East African Examinations Council
Acc. 3106	Dr Wild's report on a meeting with the Assistant Staff, 1970
Acc. 3177	Report of Commission of Inquiry into the leakage of examination papers, 1982
Acc. 3213	Queen's Award brochure 1992
Acc. 3366 JLR 36	The Present Business of UCLES, March 1988
Acc. 3366 JLR 36	Establishing a Research Facility within UCLES, summary, undated
Acc. 3366 JLR 38	Memo: Test Development and Research Unit
Acc. 3366 JLR 38	Shoesmith, D., Research and Development Provision for the Future, 1983
Acc. 3544	Financial Report 2000
A/EX 1/4	Presiding Examiners, 1901–26
A/R 4/1	TDRU (Test Development and Research Unit) Committee Minutes, 1967–8
A/WWII 1/3	Internment Camp Examinations, Singapore 1944
A/WWII 1/4	Hardships due to Air Raids, 1944
Bound Volume 1946	Examination Regulations, 1946
Bound Volume 1890–4	Examination Reports, 1893 (Juniors)
C/ACOE 2/1	Advisory Committee for Oversea Examinations Minutes, 1945–55
C/CB 3/1	Research Committee Minutes, 1939
C/R 2	Research Committee Minutes, 1947
EX/BOM	Board of Management Minutes
EX/S 1	Syndicate Minutes, various, 1970s
EX/S 3/1	Syndicate Minutes, 1931 and 1932
PP/JHF	Personal papers, James Henry Flather

PP/JNK   Personal papers, John Neville Keynes
  PP/JNK 2/1   Commonplace book
  PP/JNK 2   *Journal of Education* news cuttings
PP/JOR   Personal papers, Jack O. Roach
PP/TSW   Personal papers, Thomas S. Wyatt
  PP/TSW 3/1   Visits to Educational Testing Service, Princeton,
                     New Jersey, 1966
  PP/TSW 4/3   Reports on overseas visits made by Syndicate officers,
                     1956–65
UCLES   'Local Examinations of the University of Cambridge
                     1858–1898', The Paris Exhibit, 1900

Printed material in the Archives

Hartog, Sir Philip, 'Secondary School Examinations and the Curricula of Secondary Schools, with Suggestions for Reform'. An address to the Higher Education Meeting at the Portsmouth Conference of the National Union of Teachers, 1937 (Syndicate Room Papers (Research) box 1/8)

MEG Examiner 1994

Petch, J. A., 'JMB Standardisation and the GCE' (Nov. 1951) (PP/TSW 2/1)

'Summary of the Recommendations of the Royal Commission on Secondary Education, 1894–5' (Cambridge, 1896) (Syndicate Room Papers (Research) box 1/5)

UCLES Annual Reports (EX/AR)

UCLES pamphlet 'Standards of the Syndicate's GCE Examination' (1969) (PP/TSW 2/2)

Wyatt, T. S., 'The GCE Examining Boards and Curriculum Development' (1973) (Syndicate Room Papers (Research) box 2/30)

Cambridge University Archives

LES 1/1–6   Syndicate Minutes, 1862–1921

Cambridge University Library

Add MS 7832(1), Add MS 7840, Add MS 7835   J. N. Keynes, personal diaries

PUBLISHED SOURCES

Adeyinka, A. A., 'The Rôle of the Cambridge University Syndicate in the Development of Curriculum and Examinations in Nigerian Secondary Schools, 1910–1960 (1)', *Journal of Humanities*, 1 (Zambia, 1997), 39–59

AQA, *Setting the Standard: A Century of Public Examining by AQA and its Parent Boards* (Manchester, 2003)

Augier, R. and Irvine, D., 'Caribbean Examinations Council' in M. Bray and L. Steward, eds., *Examination Systems in Small States: Comparative Perspectives on Policies, Models and Operations* (London, 1998), 145–61

Bachman, L. F. and Palmer, A. S., *Language Testing in Practice: Designing and Developing Useful Language Tests* (Oxford, 1996)

Bardell, G. S., Forrest, G. M. and Shoesmith, D. J., *Comparability in GCE: A Review of the Boards' Studies, 1964–1977* (Manchester, 1978)

Bissoondoyal, S., 'Mauritius' in M. Bray and L. Steward, eds., *Examination Systems in Small States: Comparative Perspectives on Policies, Models and Operations* (London, 1998), 43–56

Black, M. H., *A Short History of the Cambridge University Press*, revised 2nd edn (Cambridge, 2000)

Board of Education, *Curriculum and Examinations in Secondary Schools* (London, 1943)

Bradbury, R. J., 'University of Cambridge Local Examinations Syndicate', *Magazine of the Cambridge Society*, 13 (1983), 31–8

Bray, M. and Steward, L., eds., *Examination Systems in Small States: Comparative Perspectives on Policies, Models and Operations* (London, 1998)

Brereton, J., *Exams: Where Next?* (Victoria, BC, 1965)

The Case for Examinations: An Account of their Place in Education with some Proposals for their Reform (Cambridge, 1944)

Brown, B., 'The Administration of GCSE' in R. Riding and S. Butterfield, eds., *Assessment and Examination in the Secondary School* (London, 1990), 78–103

Browne, G. F., *The Recollections of a Bishop*, 2nd edn (London, 1915)

Butterfield, S., *GCSE Objectives and Outcomes* (Examinations and Assessment Research Unit, Faculty of Education and Continuing Studies, University of Birmingham, 1989)

Daugherty, R., *National Curriculum Assessment* (London, 1995)

Edgeworth, F. Y., 'The Element of Chance in Competitive Examinations', *Journal of the Royal Statistical Society*, 53 (1890), 644–63

'The Statistics of Examinations', *Journal of the Royal Statistical Society*, 51 (1888), 599–635

Fisher, P., *External Examinations in Secondary Schools in England and Wales, 1944–1964* (Leeds, 1982)

Gosden, P. H. J. H., *Education in the Second World War: A Study in Policy and Administration* (London, 1976)

The Education System since 1944 (Oxford, 1983)

Graddol, D., *English Next* (London, 2006)

Hackett, G., 'The Most Over-tested Nation in the World', *TES*, 27 April 2001

Hartog, P. and Rhodes, E. C., *An Examination of Examinations* (London, 1935)

Howat, G., *Oxford and Cambridge Schools Examination Board 1873–1973* (Oxford, 1974)

Hughes, A., Porter, D. and Weir, C. J., eds., *ELTS Validation Project Report* (Research Report 1 (ii), British Council / UCLES, London and Cambridge, 1988)

Johnson, G., *University Politics: F. M. Cornford's Cambridge and his Advice to the Young Academic Politician* (Cambridge, 1994)

Johnson, S., *Beloe to Baker: Thirty Years of Teacher Assessment and Moderation* (Nottingham, 1989)

Kingdon, M. and Stobart, G., *GCSE Examined* (London, 1988)

McCulloch, G., 'Judgement of the Teacher: The Norwood Report and Internal Examinations', *International Studies in Sociology of Education*, 3, 1 (1993), 129–43

Mackinnon, D. and Statham, J., with Hales, M., *Education in the UK: Facts and Figures* (London, 1996)

Mathews, J. C., *Examinations: A Commentary* (London, 1985)

Messick, S. A., 'Test Validity and the Ethics of Assessment', *American Psychologist*, 35 (1980), 1012–27

Montgomery, R. J., *A New Examination of Examinations* (London, 1978)
Examinations: An Account of their Evolution as Administrative Devices in England (London, 1965)

Morris, N., 'An Historian's View of Examinations' in S. Wiseman, ed., *Examinations and English Education* (Manchester, 1961)

Nuttall, D. L., Presentation at Centre for Policy Studies Conference, 21 September in R. Murphy and P. Broadfoot, eds., *Effective Assessment and the Improvement of Education: A Tribute to Desmond Nuttall* (London, 1995), 237–41

Petch, J. A., *Fifty Years of Examining* (London, 1953)

Phillips, R. and Furlong, J., *Education, Reform and the State: Twenty-five Years of Politics, Policy and Practice* (London, 2001)

Ramsden, D., 'GCSE: The National Criteria' in K. Selkirk, ed., *Assessment at 16* (London, 1988), 16–31

Richardson, C., ed., *Whither Assessment?* (London, 2003)

Riding, R. and Butterfield, S., eds., *Assessment and Examination in the Secondary School* (London, 1990)

Roach, J., *Public Examinations in England, 1850–1900* (Cambridge, 1971)

Roach, J. O., *Some Problems of Oral Examinations in Modern Languages. An Experimental Approach Based on the Cambridge Examinations in English for Foreign Students* (Cambridge, 1945)

Rosenthal, D., 'A Day in the Life – Exams Abroad, Tyrell Smith', *CAM* (Cambridge, 1997), 31–2

Sadler, J., 'University of Cambridge Local Examinations Syndicate' in M. Bray and L. Steward, eds., *Examination Systems in Small States: Comparative Perspectives on Policies, Models and Operations* (London, 1998), 198–206

Saville, N., 'The Process of Test Development and Revision within UCLES EFL' in C. Weir and M. Milanovic, eds., *Continuity and Innovation: Revising the Cambridge Proficiency in English Examination 1913–2002* (Studies in Language Testing, 15, 2003), 57–120

Schools Council, 'A Common System of Examining at 16+', *Schools Council Examinations Bulletin* 23 (London, 1971)

Scott, D., *Coursework and Coursework Assessment in the GCSE* (CEDAR Reports 6, Warwick, 1990)

'Issues and Themes: Coursework and Coursework Assessment in the GCSE', *Research Papers in Education*, 6, 1 (1991), 3–19

Shaw, S. D. S. and Falvey, P., *The IELTS Writing Assessment Revision Project: Towards a Revised Rating Scale.* (Cambridge, 2007)

Shohamy, E. 'Language Testing: Impact' in B. Spolsky, ed., *Concise Encyclopaedia of Educational Linguistics* (Oxford, 1999), 711–14.

Smithers, A. and Robinson, P., *The Growth of Mixed A Levels* (Manchester, 1988)

Statutes and Ordinances of the University of Cambridge (Cambridge, 2006)

Stockwell, A. J., 'Examinations and Empire: The Cambridge Certificate in the Colonies, 1857–1957' in J. A. Mangan, ed., *Making Imperial Mentalities: Socialization and British Imperialism* (Manchester, 1990), 203–20

Stray, C., 'The Shift from Oral to Written Examination; Cambridge and Oxford 1700–1900', *Assessment in Education*, 8 (2001), 33–49

Sumner, L. and Archer, L., 'Bahamas' in M. Bray and L. Steward, eds., *Examination Systems in Small States: Comparative Perspectives on Policies, Models and Operations* (London, 1998), 97–105

Sutherland, G., 'The Study of the History of Education' in P. Gordon and R. Szreter, eds., *History of Education: The Making of a Discipline* (London, 1989), 73–84

Tattersall, K., 'Ringing the Changes: Educational and Assessment Policies, 1900 to the Present' in AQA, *Setting the Standard: A Century of Public Examining by AQA and its Parent Boards* (Manchester, 2003), 7–28

Taylor, L. and Falvey, P., eds., 'IELTS Collected Papers: Research in Speaking and Writing Assessment' (Studies in Language Testing, 19, forthcoming)

Thomson, D. G., *Grading Modular Curricula* (Cambridge, 1992)

UCLES, *Cambridge Examinations in English (CPE), Changes of Syllabus in 1975* (Cambridge, 1973)

Cambridge Examinations in English (CPE), Changes of Syllabus in 1984 (Cambridge, 1982)

School Examinations and their Function (Cambridge, 1976)

Valentine, C. W. and Emmet, W. G., *The Reliability of Examinations: An Enquiry* (London, 1932)

Weir, C. and Milanovic, M., eds., *Continuity and Innovation: Revising the Cambridge Proficiency in English Examination 1913–2002* (Studies in Language Testing, 15, 2003)

White, C. F., *East Midland Regional Examinations Board: A Brief History* (Nottingham, 1990)

Wiseman, S., ed., *Examinations and English Education* (Manchester, 1961)

Wood, R., *Assessment and Testing* (Cambridge, 1991)

ELECTRONIC SOURCES

ATL, '*Testing, testing, testing . . .*', *Report on Annual Conference Proceedings for April 16, 2003* at www.askatl.org.uk/atl_en/news/conferences/archive_2003/info/april_16_03/april16.asp

Evidence was also taken from interviews with, or the correspondence of, the following: J. Attwood, P. Beedle, J. Cappanera, J. Greatorex, E. Mills, T. Oates, H. Patrick, P. Stoyle.

INDEX